REFLECTIONS OF A LEGACY

THE BONNET HOUSE STORY

BY

JAYNE RICE

FOREWORD BY

S. DILLON RIPLEY

SECRETARY EMERITUS, SMITHSONIAN INSTITUTION

FEATURED PHOTOGRAPHY BY

TONY BRANCO

(ABOVE) WEDGWOOD PEDESTALED SHELL
(TITLE PAGE) BONNET LILY

EDITOR: JAYME ROBINSON; DESIGNER: WILLIAM ARMENTEROS, PRINCIPAL, DREXEL & IVES, INC.
ALL PHOTOGRAPHIC COPYRIGHTS CREDITED BY NAME. © BONNET HOUSE, INC. 1989. FORT LAUDERDALE, FLORIDA.
ALL RIGHTS RESERVED. PUBLISHED 1989. FIRST EDITION.
PRINTED IN THE UNITED STATES OF AMERICA

LIBRARY OF CONGRESS CATALOGING-IN-PUBLICATION DATA

RICE, JAYNE, 1952-   REFLECTIONS OF A LEGACY.
INCLUDES BIBLIOGRAPHICAL REFERENCES (P.   )
1. BONNET HOUSE (FORT LAUDERDALE, FLA.). 2. BARLETT FAMILY. 3. BIRCH FAMILY.
4. FORTUNE FAMILY. 5. FORT LAUDERDALE (FLA.) – BIOGRAPHY. 6. FORT LAUDERDALE (FLA.) – BUILDINGS,
STRUCTURES, ETC. 7. PAINTING, AMERICAN. 8. PAINTING – FLORIDA – FORT LAUDERDALE.
9. BONNET HOUSE MUSEUM. I. BRANCO, TONY. II. TITLE.
F319.F7R53 1989   975.9'35   89-18184

ISBN #0-9624757-0-X

CONTENTS

(ABOVE) FRESHWATER LAGOON BETWEEN THE RESIDENCE AND THE EASTERN DUNE. *(RIGHT)* S. DILLON RIPLEY

FOREWORD

S. Dillon Ripley
The Secretary Emeritus, Smithsonian Institution

*I*n the early evening when traffic has died down and the wide stretches of the beach road, A-1-A, at Fort Lauderdale are almost deserted, imagination can easily recreate the past in a long patch of dark green, feathery tree branches waving out over the west side of the erstwhile busy highway. Stand under them and look out to the calm smooth, nacreous sea. Listen, and with luck you can hear only the soughing sound, the soft murmuring of the casuarina branches overhead. So it is on the beaches of the South Pacific, rustling mostly with occasional clashing of the heavy fronds of coconut palms.

Inside, under the overhanging trees, memory carries me back to far-ago times in an Antipodean (i.e., better) world, out of sight, out of mind, the opposite of today. Turning round in my tracks to look through the trees I see the lagoon, and across it, on the rise the house, a delicious setting, like a southern plantation faced with a facade of pillars, balcony, iron bracketed grillwork, all framed within a stately array of royal palms, evenly spaced like a thin silvery diaper of stamens. Why does this seem so evocative? Perhaps because the whole assemblage of beauty was created by two pairs of hands, endlessly imaginative, creative and fun-loving. Two sets of artists' hands, crammed with the joy of living and the enthusiastic rush of fun which comes with it. Here Frederic Clay Bartlett, the distinguished artist, he of the fertile and inventive mind, trained abroad and his equally stylish and artistic wife, Evelyn Fortune created "The love-gift of a fairy tale" as Lewis Carroll once wrote. This thirty-five acres of blowing sand dunes and palmetto scrub was given as a gift by a Florida pioneer, Hugh Taylor Birch, to Mr. Bartlett and his second wife, Mr. Birch's daughter, who died after a few short years.

And now Bonnet House, risen from the dunes in the midst of Fort Lauderdale, sits serenely nestled in splendid trees, banyans, palms, gumbo-limbo and citrus, overlooking its broad sheltered lagoon, as if floating, preserved in time. This fruitful gift to Florida, an extraordinary asset to the cultural and artistic life of the center of the state for all time must live on, reminder of things past, and precursor for the coming age, a unique tribute to Evelyn Fortune Bartlett and her wholly memorable husband, Frederic, no folly this but rather a paragon beyond all praise.

(ABOVE) MAIN (SOUTH) ENTRANCE TO BONNET HOUSE. *(RIGHT)* STUDY OF BONNET HOUSE BY FREDERIC BARTLETT.

ACKNOWLEDGEMENTS

O f the many contributions to the story, those of Evelyn Fortune Bartlett were most valuable in conveying a sense of time and place at Bonnet House. Dillon and Mary Ripley and Raymond E. George fervently supported her commitment to protect and preserve Bonnet House and its personal history. The Bonnet House Book Committee, Jan Crocker, chairperson, Sandy Casteel, Pat Glenn, Sallye Jude, Edward D. Stone, Laura Ward and Barbara Keith, have guided the dream shared by many, that a pictorial commemorative book would provide a window into the romance and creativity of the Bartletts' lives. As well, the Bonnet House Alliance generously participated in this dream. Frederick Ruffner, publisher and philanthropist, has made a personal contribution. Careful research was completed by Courtney Donnell of the Art Institute of Chicago, Pamela Euston, Archivist of Bonnet House and John Craib-Cox, Chicago architectural historian. Alice Smith and Elizabeth Miller offered valuable insight in the editing process. The publishing division of the National Trust for Historic Preservation, specifically, Diane Maddex, offered helpful advice as to the process of compiling and circulating a commemorative book. The Art Institute of Chicago, The University Club of Chicago and its Archivist, Francis Dickin Weeks, and Elisabeth Bartlett Sturges, granddaughter of Frederic Bartlett, The Henry Morrison Flagler Museum in Palm Beach, Antiochiana of Antioch College, Yellow Springs, Ohio, Fairchild Tropical Garden, Coral Gables, and Flamingo Gardens, Fort Lauderdale, have willingly shared their resources with the author.

The support of all who are mentioned herein, and the Bonnet House staff, family and friends, made a meaningful difference in the progression and quality of *Reflections of a Legacy, The Bonnet House Story.*

(ABOVE) ENTRANCE GATES OPEN TO THE OASIS INSIDE. *(RIGHT)* STEPS MADE OF CORAL ROCK LEAD TO FRONT VERANDA.

INTRODUCTION
Jayne Rice

*I*magination found a new breeding ground when Frederic Bartlett received his "house lot" on the Atlantic Ocean as a wedding gift. Inspired by the philosophy noted in his personal journal, Frederic Clay Bartlett lived by a belief system that encouraged his life of creative expression: "Every human being owes a payment for being born in the world. In other words, one must pay for his birthright before one is free to follow his own selfish desires. A talented person must pay back with his talents perchance in science, engineering, architecture, painting, sculpture, in whatever branch he was endowed... ."

Bonnet House, so named to honor a yellow water "bonnet" lily growing on this "lot" in earlier years, became a home with a heart knitting three families together. In 1893, Hugh Taylor Birch discovered the southern Atlantic coast of Florida when a storm blew him to shore in the sailing vessel he had borrowed from railroad magnate Henry Flagler. Mr. Birch believed that divine forces had guided him to safety in Lake Mabel and meant him to stay in the area. His pioneering spirit found fulfillment north of Fort Lauderdale's New River Inlet, then known best by the Indians and a few local residents. When his daughter, Helen, married Frederic Bartlett in 1919, he presented them with a "house lot" from his three miles of beachfront property as a wedding gift.

Close to forty acres must have seemed like a massive canvas upon which the artist could express himself architecturally. With a worldly awareness of architectural styles, Frederic Bartlett chose to build his own interpretation of a plantation house. Once his vision was in the form of a drawing, the estate, connected by a walled courtyard, was built of local materials adapted to his design. To continue embellishing that vision after the death of Helen, his wife of six years, must have been a great struggle for Frederic. Yet the struggle was eventually overcome by the love he came to share with Evelyn Fortune, who has shaped the destiny of Bonnet House ever since.

These three families, Birch, Bartlett and Fortune, have paid back with their talents; to appreciate, protect, create and preserve not only a place, but also a set of principles by which to live. Powerful enough to nurture generations of philanthropic deeds, these principles evoke a sense of future obligation—an obligation to honor and maintain a sense of romanticism for daily life capable of reaching the still small voice within.

(ABOVE) AERIAL VIEW OF BONNET HOUSE PROPERTY. 1988. *(RIGHT)* EVELYN BARTLETT ON THE EAST VERANDA. 1988.

Bonnet House Today

A rare step into time and place is experienced by a visitor to Bonnet House, known for years in Fort Lauderdale as the Bartlett estate. Treasures enjoyed in the Bartletts' daily lives are being preserved for curious onlookers so that they may better understand the life that was led here. Romantic vision and years of labor transformed sandy dunes and marshland into a sculpted haven of beauty in which plants, animals and human beings continue to thrive. A mule named Rosie helped with chores in the fruit grove that expanded from mango and sapodilla to include guava, surinam cherry, avocado, and citrus. As the house became a winter home requiring a caretaker, butler, chef, and upstairs and downstairs maids, a quality of life was perpetuated in a colorful, original style. Playful statements in stone, concrete, wood, paint, and vegetation compose the melody of a house and environment made exceptional by the persons who have lived here.

Bonnet House in the 1980s exists in contrast to its environs—the expanding city of Fort Lauderdale, population one hundred fifty thousand, in a metropolitan area of one million. The juxtaposition of a tranquil natural environment with towering concrete structures and resort frivolities seems precarious at best. Yet, the dedication of Evelyn Fortune Bartlett to preserve the haven protected by one family's ownership for nearly one hundred years is an overwhelming gesture of philanthropy. The life and love she so delightfully shared with her artist husband, Frederic Clay Bartlett, is evidenced throughout this enchanting place.

Oceanfront living in south Florida has radically changed in one hundred years. Technology has its way of re-directing humanity. Henry Flagler's vision of a railroad linking the entire

length of Florida's east coast, now over-shadowed by jet service to major cities in the state, has brought a pace and consciousness inconceivable a century earlier. A sea of traffic flows about the Bartlett estate. Navigators on this sea seem more aware of the frenetic pace of the city than of the wonders inside the Bartlett oasis. The drumbeat of stereos along the beachside "strip," vehicles halted impatiently waiting for the drawbridge, and crowds of visitors walking the streets, all create a world that typifies the Fort Lauderdale known to most since the 1960s.

Few have the courage or the means to encapsulate time and place as the Bartletts have. There is an appeal in this oasis to all forms of life. Even a pair of monkeys from a nearby club escaped decades ago to join Frederic and Evelyn at Bonnet House. Frolicking among the network of branches and melange of foliage, the Brazilian Squirrel monkeys have grown to a colony of nearly fifty. An occasional manatee swims into the heart of the property's internal wetlands to find privacy out of the bustling Intracoastal Waterway. Turtles may be seen rising to the surface of the freshwater lagoon east of the residence to catch some moments of sunshine. Textures in botanical splendor are woven freely on the majority of the estate. But the fringes of the residence and adjoining structures show a deliberate tapestry of landscaping made possible by the addition of rich topsoil and careful plantings in an otherwise sandy environment. Seeds and seedlings of the past six decades reach high above the buildings creating a canopy that blends native and exotic flora.

The lady of Bonnet House has witnessed the fruits of her labor as she, better than anyone, has known the evolution of this environment. Her addition of black and white swans, exotic birds, the Demoiselle cranes who visit her luncheon table for a sampling of bread, and an array of flowering and fruit-bearing trees, has required a daily commitment to caring for them all. Over two thousand orchid plants promise blooms year-round, but most prolifically in Evelyn Bartlett's months of residence, December through April. All of Mother Nature has benefited from her presence and has responded most graciously to her nurturing.

Privacy has bred an aura of protection for the personal statement inside the walls of the estate. Since 1920, when construction began, only workers and invited guests were permitted to step inside, engendering curiosity in long-time residents and visitors of Fort Lauderdale. With the exception of those overly curious who were unable to resist the temptation to scale the wall to "explore," the public did

PALMS PLANTED FROM SEED EXTEND BEYOND THE SECOND STORY IN LESS THAN SIX DECADES.

not have an opportunity to experience the Bartletts' treasure until the spring of 1987, when the first guided tours were offered. Mary Ripley, a personal friend of Evelyn Bartlett and wife of the Smithsonian Institution's Secretary Emeritus, Dillon Ripley, agreed with Evelyn that the Bonnet House property should be preserved. The Ripleys suggested that the National Trust for Historic Preservation be consulted. After nearly ten years of careful planning and combined thinking directed toward finding the proper preservation plan, Evelyn Fortune Bartlett deeded the property to the Florida Trust for Historic Preservation in 1983, with a life estate. The National Trust guaranteed the preservation agreement for the property. Once a Board of Directors was established for Bonnet House, Carl Weinhardt, former Director of Villa Vizcaya in Miami and the Indianapolis Art Museum, became the first Director of Bonnet House. He carefully guided the steps taken for the private residence to become an historic house museum. Mr. Weinhardt died unexpec-

BRAZILIAN SQUIRREL MONKEYS AT PLAY.

tedly, but his concept for the guest wing at Bonnet House to become a gallery for Evelyn Bartlett's paintings was implemented soon after. This special gallery bears his name. The belief that the property should be shared with the public dovetailed with the plan for the house to become a museum. Under the subsequent directorship of Jack and Mary Wilcox, personal friends of Mrs. Bartlett, permission was granted to show the residence to visitors. Tours by reservation, conservation of the collections, and preservation of the historic site continue to be carried out by the Administrative Director and staff in concert with the Board of Directors.

MARY RIPLEY AT EVELYN BARTLETT'S
100TH BIRTHDAY CELEBRATION.

The Florida Trust for Historic Preservation has accepted the responsibility to protect the natural, historic and cultural environment that sprouted from the seeds planted by Hugh Taylor Birch nearly a century ago. This environment came to bud in Frederic Bartlett's design and flowered under the expressions of Evelyn Bartlett. Visitors taking the guided nature walk of the grounds experience their sensitivity for the environment and while touring the home, tap into the romantic way of life shared by the Bartletts and their friends. They savor for a brief time those qualities indigenous to the Florida coast before its major thrust into real estate development and tourism. For the months in which the property serves as the home of Evelyn Bartlett, her personal staff continues to maintain the order and style that has always been followed at her winter residence. In spring, summer and fall, the calendar is filled with public and privately scheduled events and educational programs. Each year however, there comes a time of great

contrast to the seasons and activities associated therein, allowing for a return to the genuine core of Bonnet House. After busloads of visitors come and go, a welcome day in time is observed in December. From a personal diary, the day is defined:

"The significance of the entire place, its essence, its space in time…its history…radiates with the clear greeting of this classic lady. Mrs. Bartlett has arrived again and we could gladly greet her via an extended hand or a kiss on the cheek. The monkeys and birds somehow knew today that she was coming—their sounds were louder than on other days; so many of them seemed to be in the courtyard. Her little dog Abbey explored the immediate area of the kitchen entrance as all persons and baggage were unloaded. It seemed to take no more than twenty minutes for her to be seated at the beautifully set table in its proper place where she would receive her lunch. Having just arrived from Massachusetts, she remained in her charcoal-gray dress adorned with the Bonnet House gold shell brooch, a favorite gold link

GALLERY OF PAINTINGS BY EVELYN BARTLETT.

INNER COURTYARD FOUNTAIN, WALKWAYS AND PLANTINGS REFLECT THOUGHTFUL DESIGN.

choker chain at her neck and a large brimmed black hat. There seems to be a peace about the home —as though it will be on its original course—the Bartlett Estate as a private residence."

Insulated from the outside world by thirty-five acres of land, Bonnet House stands in Fort Lauderdale as a symbol of respect for Mother Nature and a worldly appreciation for the Hand of Man. In its legacy lies the opportunity for future generations to experience a place begun and preserved by personal commitment and to understand the meaning in living as one believes. Architecturally, the home is Frederic Bartlett's design endowed through his past; environmentally, a vitality radiates in the flora and fauna nurtured by his wife, Evelyn; and synchronistically, their collections of paintings and objects speak of a myriad of worlds in their union. Their love and creativity is the heartbeat of Bonnet House, a heartbeat of tranquility in a city pulsing with action.

AVIARY MADE BY FREDERIC BARTLETT IN 1936
FOR THE BIRDS AND MONKEYS SO LOVED BY HIS WIFE, EVELYN.

———

CHELSEA, THE MACAW AND A CARVED OWL
FROM BALI COMPLEMENT MR. BARTLETT'S BENCH AND PAINTINGS
ALONG THE COURTYARD'S COVERED WALKWAY.

———

DEMOISELLE CRANES MOVE IN CONCERT.

———

EASTERN FACADE OF BONNET HOUSE AT EARLY MORNING.

(*LEFT*) ONE OF SPODE'S INDIAN SPORTING
DESIGNS IN A GRACEFUL ALCOVE BENEATH
A SEA TURTLE BLENDS HARMONIOUSLY WITH
OTHER ELEGANT COLLECTIBLES.

(*BELOW*) BAVARIAN CABINET HOUSES AN
APRICOT CHINA COLLECTION PAINTED WITH
COUNTRY LANDSCAPES—ALL WATCHED BY TWO
RECORD PARROT FISH.

NINETEENTH CENTURY CARVED WOODEN
MONKEY REPRESENTS A FAVORED THEME
AT BONNET HOUSE.

ELABORATE SHELLWORK AND ARTFUL BRUSHSTROKES COMBINED WITH A MEDLEY OF TREASURES
EXHIBIT THE CREATIVE FANTASY ENJOYED BY THE BARTLETTS.

COASTAL HARDWOOD HAMMOCK IS ONE OF FEW REMAINING ON FLORIDA'S EAST COAST. GUMBO LIMBO, COCO PLUM, SEAGRAPE, AND A CHAMPION PARADISE TREE RISE ABOVE AN UNDERSTORY OF WILD COFFEE, SILVER PALM AND MATURE COONTIE PLANTS.

WHITE AND BLACK SWANS
INTRODUCED BY EVELYN BARTLETT ADD
REGAL GRACE TO THE LAGOON AT BONNET HOUSE.

(BELOW) BEACHWALK
THROUGH THE HAMMOCK LEADS
TO ATLANTIC OCEAN.

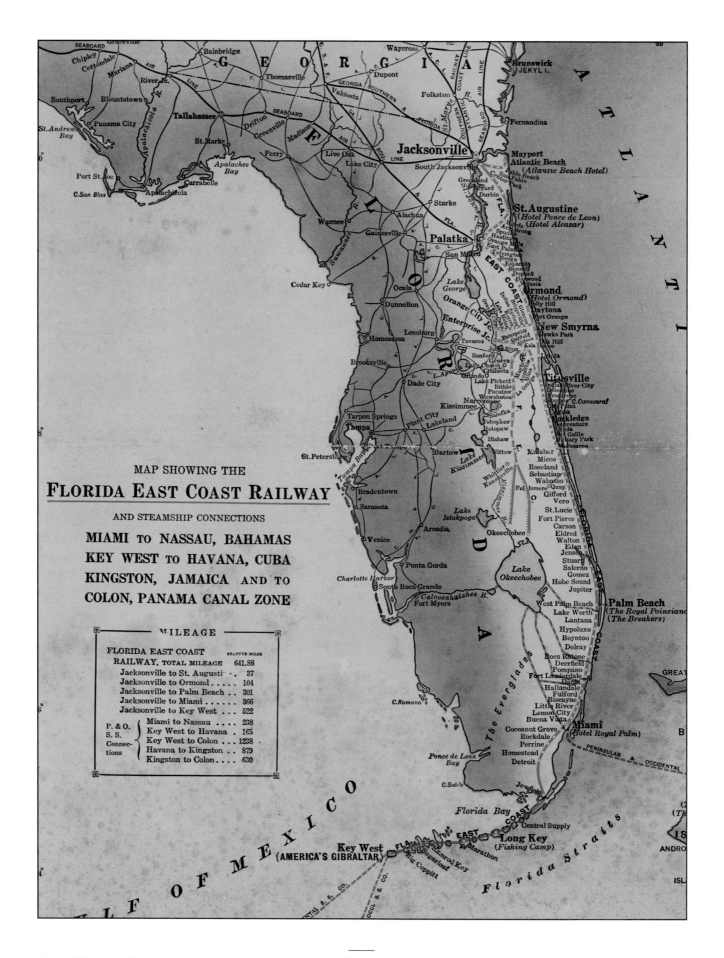

MAP SHOWING THE

FLORIDA EAST COAST RAILWAY

AND STEAMSHIP CONNECTIONS

MIAMI TO NASSAU, BAHAMAS
KEY WEST TO HAVANA, CUBA
KINGSTON, JAMAICA AND TO
COLON, PANAMA CANAL ZONE

— MILEAGE —		
FLORIDA EAST COAST		STATUTE MILES
RAILWAY, TOTAL MILEAGE		641.88
Jacksonville to St. Augustine		37
Jacksonville to Ormond		104
Jacksonville to Palm Beach		301
Jacksonville to Miami		366
Jacksonville to Key West		522
P. & O. S.S. Connections	Miami to Nassau	238
	Key West to Havana	165
	Key West to Colon	1238
	Havana to Kingston	879
	Kingston to Colon	630

(ABOVE) STATE OF FLORIDA AND ITS LINKS OF TRAVEL. CIRCA 1905. *(RIGHT)* FLORIDA PIONEER, HUGH TAYLOR BIRCH. CIRCA 1937.

A Sense of Time and Place

G olden lures to the "garden spot of the earth"[1] were being cast to Americans in the late 1800s. The climate, the low cost of land and construction, the idea of growing fruits and vegetables in the garden outside one's home, and the emergence of a railroad system that made travel in the Sunshine State possible, all merged as incentives for people to sample another side of life. Florida was also well advertised on painted railroad cars known as "The Rolling Exposition," which traveled throughout the country from 1880 to 1900 to attract public attention.[2] Henry Flagler's Florida East Coast Railway, along with its Rolling Exposition, expedited his personal mission to promote tourism along the east coast. Flagler envisioned the building of hotels and the extension of the railroad from its point of inception in Jacksonville to its southernmost destination, Key West. Henry Plant was simultaneously establishing a railroad on the west coast of Florida. While he and Flagler kept to their own coasts exclusively, both were appealing to the state legislature for the right to purchase land as their dreams to extend their railroad lines came to fruition.[3]

In 1893, the Florida East Coast Railroad stopped in Titusville. At this time, Mr. Flagler is reported to have loaned a sailing vessel to Hugh Taylor Birch, a Chicago lawyer, in the area of Hobe Sound, Florida. Mr. Birch wished to escape society's flurry as his home city was preparing for the World's Columbian Exposition. Celebrating the four hundredth anniversary of the discovery of America, the world's fair of its time caused a mass pilgrimage to Chicago. When his pet cow was put out to pasture to make room in the stall for his relatives' horses, the Florida wilderness seemed to Mr. Birch to be the only place for privacy and tranquility. He traveled by train to the

RAILROAD CARS ADVERTISED THE WAY TO
FLORIDA AS HENRY FLAGLER'S RAILWAY TRANSFORMED THE STATE.

railroad's southernmost point in Florida and boarded the boat to go further south. During an unseasonal Atlantic storm, he was carried to shore near the New River Inlet on the coast at Fort Lauderdale where the calm waters of Lake Mabel assured him: "This is where God meant me to be and this is where I will stay."[4] He soon began to purchase land at less than one dollar per acre.

Naturally, when land is acquired, a personal set of values and emotions accompanies the purchase. Mr. Birch viewed his land as a "camp" away from the social restrictions conferred upon his prominent family in a progressive American city. Here he could grow a medley of plants and fruits while preserving a segment of the natural environment that was so dear to his heart and soul. Other like-minded individuals were finding solace in south Florida for similar reasons. In 1896, Thomas Edison established his winter home on thirteen acres in the area known as Fort Myers, Florida. Robert H. Montgomery, along with Dr. David Fairchild dedicated Fairchild Tropical Garden as a public garden in 1938, on eighty-three acres south of Miami in Coral Gables. A close relationship existed between Hugh Taylor Birch and Dr. Fairchild, considered the leading American plant explorer at the turn of the century.[5] They shared correspondence, discoveries in plants that grew successfully in south Florida and reflections on development in the state, revealing a mutual respect for the land.

Mr. Birch purchased over three miles of oceanfront property and began to secure acreage inland to the west. Much of the land was marshland and swamp, and the land between the New River Sound (later, the Intracoastal Waterway) and the Atlantic coast north of the New River Inlet was considered a barrier island. It is on this parcel of land that Bonnet House would come into being. The house was named for the yellow water lily that grew prolifically in the property's marshland environment. The "bonnet lily," one of Mr. Birch's favorite flowers, remains cup-like when fully open and is also known as spatterdock. The Bonnet Slough, where the lily was found, is a curious fresh-

UPPER NEW RIVER SOUND AS SEEN BY HUGH TAYLOR BIRCH.

water source between two sand dunes bordered by saltwater perimeters. This freshwater source attracted the Indians and early explorers on the Atlantic Ocean centuries before Mr. Birch arrived. The evolution of the pristine acreage of coastal dune, marshland and swamp so treasured by Hugh Taylor Birch, created a legacy for the annals of Florida history.

As early as 1924, Hugh Taylor Birch wrote in a letter to Dr. David Fairchild, "I would love to see the land while it is yet unspoiled! To see the animals and birds and not destroy anything... The Real Estate Craze has increased ten fold."[6] The development of the Florida coast following Mr. Birch's arrival in 1893 overwhelmed him as the society from which he had hoped to escape encroached upon his private world in Fort Lauderdale. The trappings of the wealthy social circles were transforming the city of Palm Beach to the north, and George Merrick was master-planning Coral Gables in Miami, which would grow to ten thousand acres by 1925.[7] Mr. Birch described "fearful changes" taking place, all along the Florida coast south of Jupiter: "All subdivisions and many streets and small lots the prevailing fashion. No thought of tropical fruit trees and vegetation!"[8]

"Fearful changes" may best be understood when one realizes the importance of real estate in the life of Hugh Taylor Birch. Born in 1848, in Newport Township, Illinois (currently Highland Park), to Sally Milligan and Erastus Mitchell Birch, Hugh Taylor held in memory his father's gift of ten thousand acres along the Kankakee River in Indiana to Antioch College in Yellow Springs, Ohio.[9] The renowned educator, Horace Mann, had influenced Erastus to work with him at Antioch where the Birch family moved when Hugh was nine years old.[10] Wide open spaces and woodlands, coupled with the educational environment of a pro-

HELEN BIRCH LOVED SHARING THE FLORIDA WILDERNESS WITH HER FATHER, EVEN YEARS BEFORE THE BUILDING OF BONNET HOUSE.

gressive college, inspired the mind, body and soul of a boy who would support himself through three years of college in Yellow Springs before entering the legal profession in Chicago. While he did not officially graduate from Antioch until the college presented him with an honorary degree in 1929, through his work experience at the firm of Hervey, Anthony and Galt,[11] he completed the necessary credentials to be admitted to the Illinois Bar within a year.

Mr. Birch married Maria Root of Buffalo, New York, in 1876. She gave birth to three children, but within thirty-seven years of marriage all family members except Hugh Taylor and his daughter, Helen, were deceased. Their father-daughter relationship was exceptionally close since Helen's birth.[12] In the time spent together in the out-of-doors, Mr. Birch instilled in Helen an appreciation for nature which served as a source of inspiration for the poetry and music she composed. The cultural and social milieu Helen experienced in Chicago society and in her travels and studies abroad, refined the young lady to an outer and inner beauty. Society's ways did not appeal to her father and caused him to be lured away from Chicago and back to the land. Sharing "his" coastal frontier with Helen became a mutual priority as Helen elected to spend time in Florida's natural environment with her father prior to traveling to Europe to absorb its cultural riches with her mother.[13]

The Birch and Bartlett paths appear destined to have crossed as common denominators between the two old Chicago families were formulated through the years. The independent character seen in Hugh Taylor Birch likewise existed in the father of Frederic Clay Bartlett. Adolphus Clay Barlett, arriving in Chicago nearly penniless, climbed the ranks from office boy in 1864, to president of the wholesale hardware firm of Hibbard, Spencer and Bartlett by 1908. As a charter director of the Northern Trust Company in Chicago, a trustee at the Art Institute, and trustee of the University of Chicago, Adolphus held a great love for literature and art. He collected paintings and was an avid reader of the classics. With an accompanying fondness for outdoor exercise, horses and dogs, he lived a life blending modesty with tenacity as he enjoyed his quiet pleasures, supported charities, and provided a fashionable address for his family on Prairie Avenue.[14] Frederic was one of four children whose lives all revealed a cultural influence. One sister, Maie Bartlett Heard, became the founder of the Heard Museum in Phoenix, Arizona, and eventually, ran the two newspapers begun by her husband, Dwight Heard, when they moved to

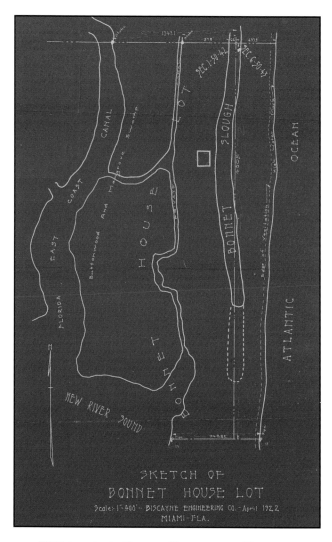

1922 SKETCH OF BONNET HOUSE LOT BY BISCAYNE ENGINEERING CO., MIAMI, FLORIDA.

Phoenix in the early 1900's. Another sister, Florence Dibell Bartlett, founded the Museum of International Folk Art in Santa Fe, New Mexico, which opened in 1953. Frederic held a sixth sense for what life had to offer and with a self-made man as his father, had a sense for holding fast to one's dreams and ambitions. Through such riches as the Chicago Symphony Orchestra and the Art Institute of Chicago, both the Birch and Bartlett families acquired a cultural base which was embellished by foreign travel and study abroad. Referring to art in so many of its forms in his personal journal, Frederic Bartlett calls "glorious music" a favorite form, and later stated, "I never realized before what depths of sorrow and what heights of joy could be attained by a piano and a few stringed instruments."[15]

Such sensitivity to music contributed to a perfect union for Frederic Bartlett and Helen Birch who were married in Boston in January of 1919. A symbolic wedding gift from the bride's father was a "house lot" amidst the beachfront acreage he owned in Fort Lauderdale. When Frederic asked, "What do you mean by a house lot?" his father-in-law, in very picturesque language answered, "Oh, as far as you can swing a cat!"[16] No doubt Mr. Birch had a very strong arm, for the house lot encompassed seven hundred feet along the ocean and thirty-five acres inland. Mr. Birch's love of the natural environment and its yield of growth and health to plants, animals and mankind was met with due respect by his family. The Bartlett family, including Mr. Birch and Frederic's son, Clay, by a former marriage, found a haven of delight and creativity away from the cold northern winters on the Florida lot. The house design incorporated studios for Helen's musical pursuits and Frederic's artistic endeavors.

Architectural design to Frederic Bartlett was not a foreign process of conceptualization.

LOW VEGETATION ON THE EASTERN DUNE PERMITTED A VIEW OF THE ATLANTIC OCEAN IN THE 1920S.

The years he spent in Europe provided a period for digestion of styles, qualities of buildings and their grounds, and the elements of design which accompany all creative processes. In addition to the many abodes that he inhabited and decorated in Munich and Paris, the residences he occupied when he returned from Europe echoed the Old World flavor. The art of the painted finish seemed to entertain the artist and his guests. With the strokes of his brush, he marbleized surfaces and created illusions in medium, subject and dimension. Painting a row of chairs along the wall of an entry hall, shrubbery on a garden wall, and convincing wood or concrete to become marble were natural expressions from the hand of Frederic Bartlett. A feeling of amusement pervades the many creative statements he made. For all who knew the man, a devotion to his own and everyone's hap-

piness around him was most genuine. In all the places he lived, the gardens contributed as much to the ambiance of the place as the interior, as though the contrast between indoors and outdoors was an essential interplay in architecture. Collections of furniture, china and art interacting with color and design of the interior were a significant part of creating his home.

The building of Bonnet House was a total architectural statement made by Frederic Clay Bartlett where he served as architect, designer, artist, and craftsman. Construction in south Florida was rapidly changing in the 1920s as private estates along the coast were becoming increasingly popular. South of Fort Lauderdale in Miami, Villa Vizcaya, the one hundred eighty acre estate of James Deering from 1916 to 1926, hinted at "America's striving for European elegance and luxury" in its formal gardens and likeness to a Venetian villa.[17] To the north, in Palm Beach, Addison Mizner had made his architectural imprint in the Mediterranean Revival style. His design and construction of the Everglades Club in 1918 catapulted his career into the world of designing private mansions that combined Old World styles with subtropical natural elements.[18] Determined not to build an Italian villa or Mizner-like creation, Frederic Bartlett planned his own idea of a plantation house. A study of Bonnet House, found sketched on the back of a menu, reveals his total thought process from individual design detail for the balcony and roofline, to the sculpted fish above the entrance archways, and elevations bordering the house. The residence was surrounded by a walled courtyard off of which the art and music studios were built. Additional buildings were constructed near the house for the caretaker, the house staff, a woodworking shop, and a storage room for tools and equipment. All materials to build the place were brought in by barge via the waterway to the west. They were transported down the dredged canal (the dog-legged slough) into the center of the property where they were unloaded and carried to the construction site. The Bartletts selected a local contractor, Samuel Drake, and builder, W.H. Rogers, who assembled their crews and started construction in 1920. All the while, Mr. Birch or Mr. Bartlett kept a watchful eye on the most personal architectural statement that they would one day call home.

As Bonnet House evolved, the talent and vision of Frederic Bartlett became evident in the eyes of all who saw it. Local curiosity was piqued during the building of the Bartlett home, and an article titled "Medieval Castle at Las Olas" appeared in the *Fort Lauderdale Sentinel* in 1921 describing the house plan as a

cross between a French villa and a medieval castle. Elaborating on the place, the reporter continued, "It is impossible to reach this castle from the ocean side on account of the fresh water slough, on the west are the tideland mud banks and mangrove tangles lining New River Sound and on the north is an almost impenetrable jungle extending to Pompano, so that south is the only approach and here one must wind his way over a sand road for nearly two miles."[19]

When imagining a sand road of arrival, the desert area amidst the south drive was a natural landscape for the approach to the main entrance of the house. Maintaining the sandy desert environment was considered appropriate for a Florida home, and the grounds remained as prominent in Frederic's mind as the building design. This is evidenced by the compatibility of landscape and architecture. As materials were arriving by barge on the canal to

HELEN AND FREDERIC BARTLETT
AT SOUTH ENTRANCE OF BONNET HOUSE. CIRCA 1922.

the west, a well-designed plan for Florida living was coming to life. All rooms of single depth allowed air flow to pass through and bless the inhabitants with Florida's coastal breezes. The enclosed courtyard with covered walkways created a private garden area to enjoy, rain or shine. As the structure emerged, space was translated into place through design and use of materials indigenous to the area. Coral rock was used as inlay in the outlining arch detail of the tower, and to create the original courtyard fountain, walkways, and the pair of obelisks as entrance sculpture. Cypress saplings for roof structure and "Dade County pine" for interior detail were the local lumbers used, while sand was combined with other raw materials to pour the concrete block right on the construction site. Inlaid shells in the concrete complemented by mounted fish hanging on the walls of the dining room echo the ocean's proximity to the house. Large verandas adjacent to the drawing and dining rooms, and the covered balcony wrapped around the second floor, correspond with Frederic's interpretation of a plantation house, further embellished with ironwork from New Orleans for the balustrades.

———

JUNGLE MURAL SCENE PAINTED BY FREDERIC BARTLETT AT THE HOME OF ROBERT ALLERTON IN 1927.

Through the years of Frederic's marriage to Helen, Bonnet House had a less formal style in comparison to other beachfront homes of its era. To Mr. Birch and the Bartletts, privacy may have equalled the importance of the temperate climate, for their winter retreat provided a place to live a wholesome, simple and happy life. Work was pleasurable for all — Mr. Birch worked on clearing land, Frederic painted and created, Helen wrote poetry and music, and Clay played the saxophone and attended school north of Fort Lauderdale at the Hillsborough Academy. When the family was away from Bonnet House, they were often together traveling in Europe, the Mediterranean, Egypt and islands close to home. With such fullness of life, there is little wonder that the loss of Helen affected everyone deeply. Helen died suddenly of cancer in the fall of 1925, within months of Mr. Birch and Frederic purchasing a summer home for the family in Beverly, Massachusetts. Work and creativity diminished on the Bonnet House property during the following five years as the sense of home was altered. To pass the time, Mr. Birch continued clearing the land, and because Frederic and his son were often away traveling, he spent many weeks alone in Florida. Nearly two years after Helen's death, Mr. Birch wrote to Dr. Fairchild during a lonesome time: "Mr. Bartlett has been all winter in Europe — from France through Holland, Denmark, Sweden, Germany and England and back to Boston and Chicago and is now with our friend Robert Allerton in his palatial home at Monticello, Illinois, where Frederic is doing some fine mural work and will be there until we both go back to Beverly, Massachusetts, about the 15th of May."[20] Both men, however, would carry on through long lives, committed to that in which they believed and driven by their passions; the land for Hugh Taylor Birch and art for Frederic Bartlett.

CLAY BARTLETT, HUGH TAYLOR BIRCH, HELEN AND FREDERIC BARTLETT. CIRCA 1924.

FRONT VERANDA OF BONNET HOUSE, 1920S.

FRONT VERANDA OF BONNET HOUSE, 1980S.

OCTAGONAL INTERIOR WITHIN A RECTANGULAR EXTERIOR IS FACED IN CYPRESS, ADDING WARMTH TO THE DINING ROOM.

"…A KNAPSACK OF ANTIQUE STEINS PURCHASED…
IN THE LITTLE STOWED-AWAY VILLAGE WHERE I HAD BEEN WORKING…"
FREDERIC BARTLETT, AFTER A WEEK'S SKETCHING TRIP
IN THE COUNTRY OUTSIDE OF MUNICH.

——

——

A PAIR OF FISH ATOP AN ELABORATELY
INCISED PEDESTAL IS FROM THE COLLECTION OF
HELEN AND FREDERIC BARTLETT.

——

——

TROMPE-L'OEIL BALUSTRADE OF THE STUDIO BALCONY EVEN SURPRISED FRANK LLOYD WRIGHT
WHEN HE VISITED HIS FRIEND FREDERIC BARTLETT.

THE STUDIO RESEMBLES A MUSEUM OF STILL LIFE OBJECTS.

THE ART STUDIO OF FREDERIC BARTLETT. 1989.

STUDIO'S GREAT NORTH WINDOW PROVIDES THE
PERFECT LIGHT IN WHICH TO PAINT.

———

MUSIC ROOM WITH PATTERNED FLOOR PAINTED BY FREDERIC BARTLETT. FURNISHINGS FROM HELEN BIRCH BARTLETT
WERE ENHANCED BY ADDITIONS OF EVELYN BARTLETT.

———

MUSIC ROOM INTERIOR. CIRCA 1924.

VEILED LADY.
MARBLE BUST BY ITALIAN SCULPTOR,
GIUSEPPE CROFF.

"ROSIE'S PALACE"—BARN NAMED AFTER MR. BIRCH'S MULE.

———

East entrance to courtyard adorned by cowfish floating in a sea of blue.

SERVICE BUILDINGS INCLUDED RESIDENCES FOR THE HOUSE STAFF AND MANY
GARAGES FOR TOOLS, EQUIPMENT AND VEHICLES.

———

CARETAKER'S QUARTERS WAS ORIGINALLY THE TWO-STORY PORTION OF THE EXISTING BUILDING.

TIMETABLE

1893-95: CHARCOAL SKETCH
BY FREDERIC BARTLETT

1920: BONNET HOUSE CONSTRUCTION BEGINS

1893: COVER OF WORLD'S COLUMBIAN
EXPOSITION BOOK OF PHOTOGRAPHS

CIRCA 1935: *DOUBLE VASE*
BY EVELYN BARTLETT

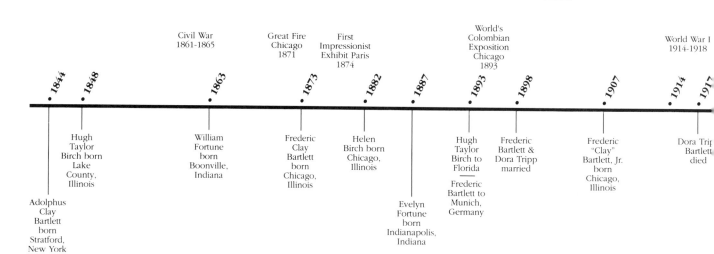

Civil War
1861-1865

Great Fire
Chicago
1871

First
Impressionist
Exhibit Paris
1874

World's
Columbian
Exposition
Chicago
1893

World War I
1914-1918

1844 1848 1863 1873 1882 1887 1893 1898 1907 1914 1917

Hugh
Taylor
Birch born
Lake
County,
Illinois

William
Fortune
born
Boonville,
Indiana

Frederic
Clay
Bartlett
born
Chicago,
Illinois

Helen
Birch born
Chicago,
Illinois

Hugh
Taylor
Birch to
Florida

Frederic
Bartlett to
Munich,
Germany

Frederic
Bartlett &
Dora Tripp
married

Frederic
"Clay"
Bartlett, Jr.
born
Chicago,
Illinois

Dora Trip
Bartlett
died

Adolphus
Clay
Bartlett
born
Stratford,
New York

Evelyn
Fortune
born
Indianapolis,
Indiana

CIRCA 1925: *SWEDISH BAR (PARIS)*
BY FREDERIC BARTLETT

1938: BOTHWAYS FARM PURCHASED

1982: FREDERIC CLAY BARTLETT MEMORIAL GALLERY
ENDOWED BY EVELYN FORTUNE BARTLETT

1926: GIFT TO THE ART INSTITUTE OF CHICAGO
BEDROOM AT ARLES BY VINCENT VAN GOGH

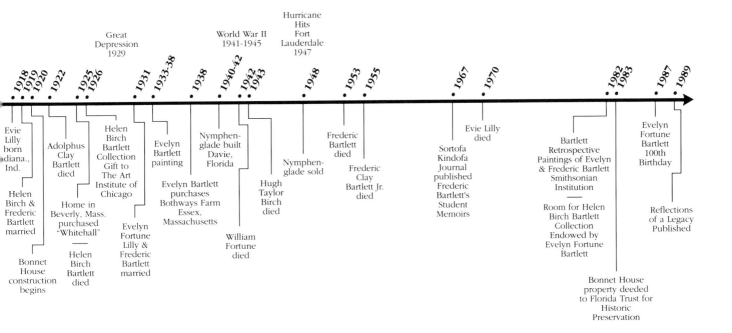

(ABOVE) UNTITLED OIL ON CANVAS BY FREDERIC CLAY BARTLETT. CIRCA 1935.
(RIGHT) FREDERIC BARTLETT, 1922.

A Talent Established

"All passes—ART alone endures."[1] To Frederic
Clay Bartlett, art would always be the enduring quality in his life. The 1893 World's Columbian
Exposition, ironically the same event that had prompted his future father-in-law to escape from
Chicago, was an artistic revelation for Frederic. Exposure to the cultural riches of nations around
the world had whet his appetite to experience the world outside of Chicago. Years following this
extravaganza, Frederic recalled this turning point as he wrote his personal memoir titled *Sortofa
Kindofa Journal of My Own*: "Tired we were, for as was our custom, we had walked past miles
and miles of pictures, a never-ending wild excitement for us. To think that men could conceive
such things, and actually bring them into being on a flat bare canvas: Could create illusions of
space, perspective, sunlight or storm, all on a piece of bare canvas. ..."[2] Shortly thereafter, at age
nineteen, he left for Europe to study, pledging himself "to the creation of beauty and determined
to leave the luxury of home, ... to learn the technique, secrets and methods of artists."[3]

Frederic Bartlett was one of a host of American painters who in the late 1800s, looked to
Europe for a level of training that was unattainable in America. After studying and apprenticing
with the masters, these artists returned to America to become part of the "technically best-trained
generation in the history of American art."[4] At this time, a great segment of American society was
becoming disillusioned in a nation that was growing rich and more industrialized. Not only
painters, but writers, architects and art collectors were turning to Europe for their answers and
ideals.[5] A growing interest in Impressionism and its philosophy that works of art no longer
needed to imitate or represent natural objects and events was changing perspective in the art

"WHITE COLUMNS AGAINST AN INLAND SEA…"
FREDERIC BARTLETT. WORLD'S COLUMBIAN EXPOSITION, 1893.

world everywhere.[6] Yet an underlying academic training was still considered essential, and Frederic Bartlett held firmly to this belief.

Acceptance at the Royal Academy in Munich was a notable honor for any American, and by 1896, Frederic Bartlett would receive his degree from the Academy. Living in a foreign city added first hand exposure to European tastes and lifestyle. Of all the places he would live, Munich, and its spirited Bavarian culture, was the one he loved most. After leaving Munich, he continued his academic training in Paris at the Ecole Collin for drawing, Aman-Jean's School for painting, and the Academie Colarossi for figure drawing.[7] When James McNeill Whistler began his "short-lived Paris studio, Bartlett was one of the first to enroll."[8] Studying with Whistler, a forerunner of Impressionist painting in England and America, was considered a great opportunity to students of painting and drawing and Frederic Bartlett ever remembered his criticisms from the master.

The prominent muralist, Puvis de Chavannes, was one of Frederic Bartlett's most influential and honored mentors. Although Mr. Chavannes' involvement in monumental works for Paris, Boston and Marseilles precluded Frederic's studying with him, the muralist did spend time with Frederic as he enlarged his sketches to mural scale.[9] Criticisms from Chavannes inspired Frederic Bartlett's lifelong passion for mural design and painting, on both a private and public level. Italian classical elements, German symbols, medieval subjects, depth of color, and an overall fascination with antiquity and foreign customs filter through the brush strokes of an artist who had opened himself to the world.

Having met his bride-to-be in Munich four years earlier, Frederic Bartlett married Dora Tripp of White Plains, New York, in 1898. Although he believed "one never finishes one's education,"[10] he spent his "final" year as a student with Dora in Paris and in Munich before taking up residence in Chicago. They built Dorfred House, named for the two of them, on Prairie Avenue where Frederic had lived as a child.[11] Here, Frederic incorporated into the interior many of the objects of art and architectural ornamentation they had collected in Europe. Trompe-l'oeil shrubbery and pedestals supporting grotesque classic masks greeted visitors in the entry vestibule. Attached to rooms painted with swags of fruit, garlands, and fanciful animals of a Renaissance spirit, the studio stretched across the entire rear of the house, nearly forty by twenty-five feet, to accommodate the large scale murals of the artist's career.[12] Frederic also held a studio address in the Fine Arts Building on South Michigan Avenue, "Chicago's mecca of artistic activities."[13]

Commissions flowed to Frederic Bartlett, oftentimes in collaboration with architects. He always integrated painting, architecture and decoration in his work,[14] giving him the opportunity to work with other professionals. In 1900, with architect Howard Van Doren Shaw, he completed twenty-five frescoes of angels

CHARCOAL SKETCH COMPLETED BY FREDERIC BARTLETT AT THE ROYAL ACADEMY IN MUNICH, 1895.

"House in the Woods," Lake Geneva, Wisconsin. Architect Howard Shaw and Frederic Bartlett collaborate to create the home of Adolphus Clay Bartlett. 1906.

singing and playing medieval instruments and a monumental "Tree of Life" mural in the chancel of the Second Presbyterian Church on South Michigan Avenue.[15] Five years later, he and Shaw combined their creative forces to design and build a home for his father, Adolphus Clay Bartlett in Lake Geneva, Wisconsin. The "House in the Woods," situated amidst thirty-six acres of woodlands bordering on the lake, is appropriately named. The U-shaped residence is designed around an inner courtyard with an artist's studio at the courtyard's end. Considered a most whimsical architectural statement by Shaw, the home was obviously influenced by Frederic Bartlett's creative spirit. Elegantly featured in *Ladies Home Journal* in 1909, "House in the Woods" is described as an Italian plan containing many suggestions of early German work and modern Munich.[16] Throughout the life of Frederic Clay Bartlett, a serendipitous personal style would continue to evolve.

The building boom in Chicago near the turn of the century was "accompanied by a great demand for decorative art in public buildings."[17] Frederic was commissioned to do a richly-gessoed frieze depicting medieval athletic games in the Frank Dickinson Bartlett Memorial Gymnasium at the University of Chicago named in honor of Frederic's brother.[18] He also worked with the architect Martin Roche, designing the interior of the University Club, Chicago's earliest building to serve men of many an alma mater. The Gothic feeling in this thirteen-story structure is epitomized in the dining area, Cathedral Hall. Frederic Bartlett's designs for fourteen stained glass windows, each three stories in height, were selected over those of Louis Comfort Tiffany to grace the room with color and design. "A Gothic Chase and Feast," the medieval theme he painted on the ceiling panels of the Club's Michigan Room, meets harmoniously with the Gothic style of the walnut-paneled room. The palette, subject matter and style in his subsequent murals at the Fourth Presbyterian Church and in the Fine Arts Building, portray the qualities seen in many of his Chicago commissions. Whether classical, medieval, primitive, or whimsical, the many expressions of Frederic Bartlett were left as reminders of a living talent throughout his home city.

As a member in the National Institute of Arts and Letters, trustee at the New York Museum of Modern Art and trustee at the Art Institute of Chicago,[19] Frederic Bartlett kept his finger on the pulse of the art world. When he began to work on canvasses at an easel, the themes of his paintings became more personal and a strong influence of Impressionism and Post-Impressionism was evident. For a brief period in the 1930s, even the effects of Cubism influenced his work. The Art Institute of Chicago gave several one-man shows honoring Frederic Bartlett, and a sampling of his works remains in their permanent collection. Other works are found at the Corcoran Gallery in Washington, D.C., the Carnegie Institute in Pittsburgh, and in private collections.

MAGAZINE COVER FEATURING
"CANTON STREET" BY F.C. BARTLETT. PAINTING IN
THE CORCORAN GALLERY OF ART COLLECTION.

Although Frederic Bartlett was a prolific painter until his cataract operation in 1932, the artist considered himself more of a collector than an artist. In his student years, the joy of discovering furnishings, art objects, and decorative touches for the places he lived, launched his enthusiasm for collecting. Antique shops and flea markets in Europe offered intriguing treasures of the Old World. Creating homes in Europe delighted him as he blended collections with enchanting interior and exterior spaces. His passion for artistry and collecting would continue throughout his life, and he shared this enthusiasm with those he loved.

Dora and Frederic Bartlett enjoyed nineteen years of marriage, from the student years through the years of public art exhibits and commissions. Their only son, Clay, shared in the arts and travel with the family. Clay's paintings, known best in the New England world of painting, are represented in the collections at Bonnet House. Dora died in 1917, when Clay was only ten years old, leaving Frederic and his son alone. In two years, Frederic married Helen Birch and continued the creative life he had already begun, but on new horizons.

FOURTH PRESBYTERIAN CHURCH IN CHICAGO. CEILING PANELS PAINTED BY FREDERIC BARTLETT. 1914.

CATHEDRAL HALL AT THE UNIVERSITY CLUB OF CHICAGO.
FOURTEEN STAINED GLASS WINDOWS WERE
DESIGNED BY FREDERIC BARTLETT. 1908. MEDALLIONS ABOVE WINDOWS
FROM MUNICH, GERMANY, ADDED BY MR. BARTLETT IN 1916.

———

DETAIL: WINDOW OF MUSIC
SEVEN WINDOWS REPRESENT COLLEGE DISCIPLINES THAT LEAD TO PROFESSIONAL CAREERS—
LITERATURE, LAW, SCIENCE, RELIGIONS, THE ARTS, MUSIC AND COMMERCE.

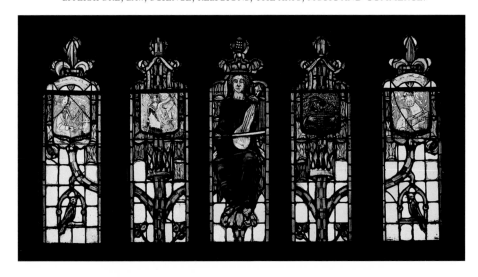

Five windows contain seals of sixty-five colleges or universities attended by many members of the club. Two windows represent the U.S. Navy and U.S. Army.

DETAIL: MEDIEVAL FEAST. ONE OF FIFTY-SIX CEILING PANELS PAINTED
BY FREDERIC BARTLETT IN 1909.

———

MICHIGAN ROOM: UNIVERSITY CLUB OF CHICAGO. CEILING PANELS DEPICT *A GOTHIC CHASE AND FEAST.*

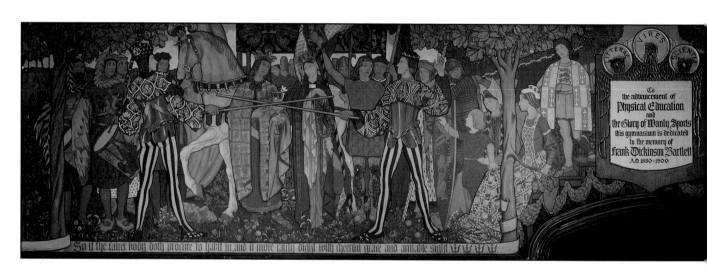

RICHLY GESSOED FRIEZE DEPICTING MEDIEVAL GAMES FOR
THE FRANK DICKINSON BARTLETT GYMNASIUM, UNIVERSITY
OF CHICAGO. 1904.

———

Within the mural:

LITTERA · VIRES · SCIENTIA

To
the advancement of
Physical Education
and
the Glory of Manly Sports
this gymnasium is dedicated
to the memory of
Frank Dickinson Bartlett
A.D. 1880 · 1900

How happy is he born and taught that serveth not another's will; whose armour is his honest thought & simple truth his utmost skill.

BROTHER OF FREDERIC BARTLETT, FRANK D. BARTLETT DIED
IN 1900 WHILE A STUDENT AT HARVARD. THEIR FATHER
ENDOWED THE GYMNASIUM AS A MEMORIAL.

———

MURAL BY F.C. BARTLETT (1910) ON TENTH FLOOR OF FINE ARTS
BUILDING, CHICAGO, LOCATION OF MR. BARTLETT'S STUDIO.

———

SECOND PRESBYTERIAN CHURCH, CHICAGO. TREE OF LIFE MURAL PAINTED BY F.C. BARTLETT IN 1900.

CHINESE TEMPLE I BY F.C. BARTLETT. CIRCA 1925.

CHINESE TEMPLE II BY F.C. BARTLETT. CIRCA 1925.

A MUSICAL INTERPRETATION BY FREDERIC BARTLETT. CIRCA 1935.

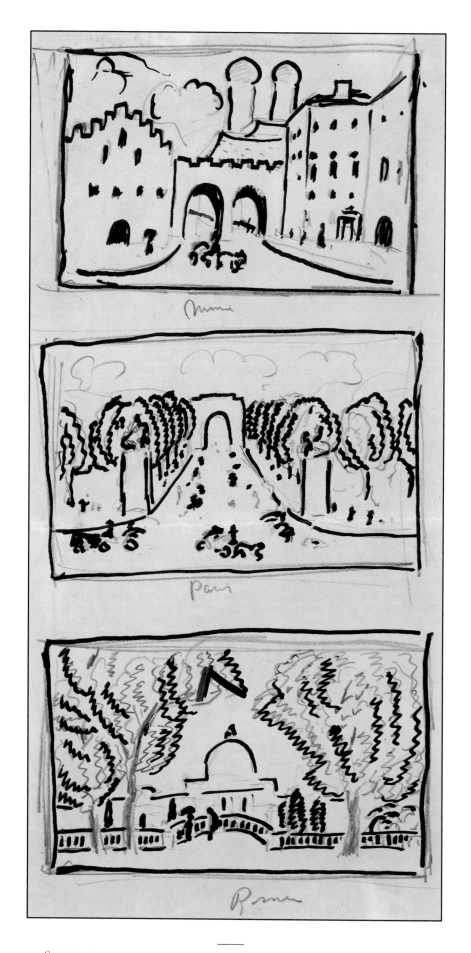

SKETCHES OF FOREIGN CITIES CLOSE TO THE HEART OF FREDERIC BARTLETT.

(ABOVE) GLEN HELEN, 800 ACRES OF WOODLANDS IN YELLOW SPRINGS, OHIO, GIVEN IN MEMORY OF HELEN BIRCH BARTLETT
BY HER FATHER. *(RIGHT)* HELEN BIRCH BARTLETT. CIRCA 1921.

INFLUENCE IN HARMONY

*T*he delight of life! That was Helen Birch's precious gift, both to give and to receive. She had always wanted people to express life as they really saw it, unsentimentalized and unshadowed by tradition, and this at once made rational to her the new forms in music, letters and painting ..."[1] Helen was both a published composer and poet. *Poetry Magazine* and a Chicago music company published her songs, settings for poems, book reviews and poetry. In 1927, a book of her collected poems, entitled *Capricious Winds*, was published.[2]

The memory of Helen Birch Bartlett triggered many inspirational gifts highlighted by the "well-watered woodland of Glen Helen"[3] at Antioch College from her father and a collection of Post-Impressionist paintings at the Art Institute of Chicago from her husband. Hugh Taylor Birch found some peace in knowing that such earthly riches as the woodlands would echo his love for his daughter. In later years, he named a lake for her on his Florida parcel of land. That parcel would eventually be given to the state as a park. Frederic too, found solace in knowing that a world renowned art collection would commemorate his beloved wife.

The paintings acquired by Frederic and Helen for a later donation to a major museum reveal a combined vision in their years as collectors and world travelers. The life of collecting that had begun when Frederic Bartlett was a student at the Royal Academy in Munich became more sophisticated during his marriage to Helen Birch. After their marriage, they received one of the first visas to go to China following World War I.[4] Their predominately European collection grew to include the Orient. Chinese porcelains and Oriental lacquered and paper screens were

THE BASKET OF APPLES BY PAUL CEZANNE. 1895.

———

brought back to add to the interiors of their homes. Subject matter in Frederic's paintings on canvas includes scenes from the Orient and exhibits a style of refinement more closely related to his works done in the Academy. When in France, following the era of Impressionism, exposure to the avant-garde works of art became a foremost attraction for both Helen and Frederic. In the context of European and American taste for modern art in the mid 1920's, the Bartletts were among several dozen courageous collectors who had the foresight and finances to acquire many great masterpieces.[5] Their collection, first exhibited at the Art Institute of Chicago in 1923, preceded any other permanent display of modern art in a public gallery in America.[6] Considered a most notable event in the lives of Frederic and Helen Bartlett, and the most important acquisition in the history of the Art Institute of Chicago, the purchase of George Seurat's *Sunday Afternoon on the Island of La Grande Jatte* was one of the most significant gifts to the world of modern art in America.[7]

Having been appointed to succeed his father as a trustee of the Art Institute in 1923, Frederic had a well-aimed concern for the museum and the quality of its collections. As other major works were added to their collection, including those of Van Gogh, Matisse, Gauguin, and Cezanne, the paintings were exhibited at the Art Institute and in Boston and Minneapolis under the name the Birch-Bartlett Collection of Modern French Paintings.[8] Upon the untimely death of Helen Birch Bartlett, Frederic arranged to present the collection as a memorial gift to the Art Institute of Chicago. Steps were taken to refine the content of the collection to twenty-four masterpieces. Several minor paintings were sold, and works by Van Gogh, Toulouse-Lautrec, Gauguin, Rousseau and Picasso were added.[9]

For the Bartletts, modern art was essentially Post-Impressionist figure painting brought forward into the twentieth century.[10] The desire to have representative works of each major "genre" explored by the masters of late nineteenth and early twentieth century painting is evident in the pattern of their purchases. From Helen's death in October 1925, until February of 1928, Frederic Bartlett spent over $100,000 on the collection before concerning himself with its pictorial unity. Selecting frames, correct moldings, colors, and spacings, he left his mark on the presentation of this private collection so that it would remain together harmoniously as a memorial to his wife.[11]

In the closeness that remained between Frederic Bartlett and Hugh Taylor Birch for the rest of their lives, one senses the bond that was created in the joy and tragedy of their worlds intertwined with Helen's. The giving and receiving that characterized her life, has, and will continue to enlighten the world through the environment in which she is memorialized.

AT THE MOULIN ROUGE BY HENRI DE TOULOUSE-LAUTREC. 1892.

TAHITIAN WOMAN WITH CHILDREN BY PAUL GAUGUIN. 1901.

DAY OF THE GODS (MAHANA NO ATUA) BY PAUL GAUGUIN. 1894.

SUNDAY AFTERNOON ON THE ISLAND OF LA GRANDE JATTE
BY GEORGES SEURAT. 1884-86.

———

THE OLD GUITARIST BY PABLO PICASSO. 1903.

THE WATERFALL (LA CASCADE) BY HENRI ROUSSEAU. 1910.

———

MADAME ROULIN ROCKING THE CRADLE
(LA BERCEUSE)
BY VINCENT VAN GOGH. 1889.

———

(ABOVE) APPLE BANANAS AND SEA FAN, WATERCOLOR BY EVELYN BARTLETT. CIRCA 1932.
(RIGHT) EVELYN BARTLETT WITH WHITE BIRD. CIRCA 1935.

A COMMITMENT NURTURED

$\mathcal{M}$erging the creative energy of two individuals appears providential when one senses the reach of their combined talent. Having lived through substantial personal histories prior to meeting one another, Frederic Bartlett and Evelyn Fortune Lilly had a refined appreciation for what they wanted in life by the mid 1920s. A cousin of Helen Birch Bartlett, Catharine Beveridge (wife of Indiana's Senator Albert J. Beveridge), had offered a summer residence in Beverly Farms, Massachusetts, to Evelyn and her daughter, Evie, following Evelyn's divorce from Eli Lilly of the pharmaceutical family. The Birch-Bartlett family summered in Beverly where they made the acquaintance with Evelyn and her daughter. Following the death of Helen, the acquaintance became a friendship that brought new life to both Frederic and Evelyn. The genteel demeanor of Frederic Bartlett and his concern for happiness in others disarmed the shyness Evelyn had experienced in her life. In all of his years of artistic endeavor, Frederic Bartlett considered his most successful artistic venture to be the discovery of the art of Evelyn Bartlett.[1]

Frederic and Evelyn Bartlett were married on June 1, 1931, at the country home of the bride's father, William Fortune.[2] Mr. Fortune, a philanthropic gentleman of international recognition and civic leader in his hometown of Indianapolis, Indiana, most humbly received great respect from all who knew him. His dedication to standing for what one believes in set the example for a parallel commitment in his daughter. The middle child of three, Evelyn was born September 30, 1887, to May Knubbe and William Fortune. Since childhood, Evelyn has had a "sixth sense" for correctness — an order for placement, for presentation, a sense of accuracy coupled with an appreciation for beauty. Other than a brief session of Saturday morning art classes focused on sketching, she had no formal art training in her background. This sense of correctness is not limited to drawing as it carries through into needlework, sewing and flower arranging. Having learned to work well with her hands before the age of twelve, Evelyn Bartlett has held to the belief that young people should learn to work with their hands at an early age.

As talent stems from an innate depth in Evelyn Fortune Bartlett, so too does a sensitivity to the riches of Mother Nature. Growing up in the Indianapolis neighborhood of Woodruff Place, still a woodland at the time, she experienced a Renaissance style found in the community's fountains, esplanades and statuary. Playing in the woodlands and freshness of the outdoors gave her a healthy appreciation for

PORTRAIT OF CATHARINE BEVERIDGE
BY EVELYN FORTUNE BARTLETT. CIRCA 1935.

———

life. The loss of her mother at age eleven left her guidance to her father, an aunt and a grandmother. She became well-versed in academics as well as in social graces. She attended the private girls' school of Knickerbacker Hall in Indianapolis. Following her secondary education and according to her father's wishes, she went to Pleasantville, New York, where she attended the finishing school of Briarcliff, located near the Hudson River.

Talent and sensitivity in the life of Evelyn Fortune found a kindred spirit in Frederic Clay Bartlett. Shortly after her marriage to Frederic, the talents of Evelyn Bartlett converged on palette and paper, then canvas. At the

time of her husband's recovery from a cataract operation, she sketched his folded hands, and her attention to exactness was recognized by his healing artistic eye. While painting would never be the same for Frederic after the operation, his encouragement of Evelyn would catapult her into a world of color, design and texture on a painted surface. Her choice of subject matter reflects her favorite elements in life; close friends, family and special little dogs; color and texture; and design found in daily life, including flowers, shells and books. From the time she met Frederic, a small dog has accompanied her and has appeared in many of her paintings.

She first experimented with watercolor and found that it could easily be transported while traveling. The Bartletts reserved a salon on board the Canadian National Steamships, "Lady Boats," which traveled to Bermuda, Nassau, and Jamaica via the St. Lawrence River.[3] This trip provided the opportunity to focus on the riches of the tropics. After buying a large basket of fruit on one of the islands, Frederic describes the longevity of the produce: "Mrs. Bartlett painted ten water colors. Then I was free to eat the fruit. As still further proof of our economy, we saved the seeds and have planted them on our Florida place."[4]

Traveling in the islands during the winter confirmed for the Bartletts that they would enjoy taking up seasonal residence at the Florida estate that was begun a decade earlier in Fort Lauderdale. Through the romance and creativity shared by the Bartletts, Bonnet

House would undergo a renaissance which came to govern its destiny. Architectural embellishments were selected through the years, transforming the home's form and function to an aesthetically-pleasing residence. Bay windows were added to the eastern facade of the home, brightening the drawing room and master bedroom suite. Working together, the two artists painted the walls and woodwork, and added to the architectural detail. Frederic's faux marble painting traveled throughout the home and is epitomized in the trompe l'oeil balustrade in his art studio. Ceiling murals were painted in each of the three courtyard loggias, the last of which was graced by Evelyn's brush. On top of a scaffold, Frederic painted the shells, fish and turtle in the mural, then asked his wife to add the rope-like netting over his entire composition.

PAIRS, WATERCOLOR BY EVELYN BARTLETT. CIRCA 1932.

Although Evelyn needed little guidance in her painting, Frederic did show her the arrangement of pigments on a palette and made occasional suggestions for backgrounds in her portraits. She continued to paint in oils on canvas at Bonnet House, where the portraits of her father and Mr. Birch were completed. Her father spent six weeks of the winter at the Boca Raton Club north of Fort Lauderdale and visited the Bartletts each afternoon to keep in touch with their creative ventures. For many years, Mr. Birch shared in the life at Bonnet House with Frederic and Evelyn until he built his own residence in "the Oaks," just north of the Bonnet House property (later to be Birch State Park).

EVELYN AND FREDERIC BARTLETT ON HONEYMOON ABOARD THE BREMEN LINE TO EUROPE. 1931.

Evelyn Bartlett painted for a period of five years between 1933 and 1938. Frederic had arranged three showings of her work at the Galleries of Wildenstein & Co. in New York, the John Heron Art Museum in Indianapolis and at their studio in Beverly, Massachusetts. Throughout the period of public exposure of her paintings, Evelyn Fortune Bartlett received good criticisms. Her husband wrote of her brief period of working with a brush as "small moment, for the works themselves show that painting has been going on with eye and mind most of her life."[5]

In their years together at Bonnet House, the Bartletts inspired one another in the creation of their own subtropical wonderland. As the city around them stretched to accommodate automobiles and more visitors, their commitment to preserving a haven of privacy strengthened. Frederic built a wall when he realized that a beach road would eventually be built between his home and the Atlantic Ocean. The wall established the western-most boundary for Atlantic Boulevard, later known as State

PORTRAIT OF WILLIAM FORTUNE BY HIS DAUGHTER.
CIRCA 1935.

Road A-1-A, and a fence was extended the length of the property's eastern edge. Cutting off direct access to the beach, the Bartletts decided to transform the marshy, freshwater slough in front of their home into a lagoon tipped with ponds at either end. When dredging was completed, an allee between each pond and the lagoon seemed a natural addition reminiscent of the tree-lined promenades so familiar to Frederic in Europe. With a birthday check received from her father, Evelyn added royal palms to grace the lagoon's borders with stature. The thatched roof bridge was reconstructed by an area Seminole Indian family to provide a way across the water to the eastern dune. With traffic infringing on the beach, the idyllic environment at Bonnet House became more important to the shore birds, turtles, and the fish and swans added by the Bartletts.

Even when mixed with the little dogs of honor, pet monkeys and exotic birds have found delight in their home at Bonnet House. Evelyn Bartlett's love of animals, so akin to that in Hugh Taylor Birch, added new dimension to Frederic's creative pursuits in the building of the carnival-like aviary for the courtyard. To be used for her monkeys or her birds, this fanciful house and its inhabitants blended ideally with the whimsy filtered throughout the home. Frederic's carousel collection, a menagerie in its own right, was placed in the same courtyard with Evelyn's collection of carved wooden animals from the South Sea Islands, adding the "finishing touches" along the covered walkways and verandas.

All residents of Bonnet House thrive in the thirty-five acres of natural environment. As a wedding gift to Frederic and Evelyn, Mr. Birch gave an additional one hundred feet of land to the south of the original property and later gave them one hundred feet to the north.[6] For the environment to accommodate a more ex-

BAY WINDOWS ADDED TO THE DRAWING ROOM OPENED THE INTERIOR TO THE OUT-OF-DOORS.

otic vegetation, the Bartletts requested professional guidance from the head gardener at the Boca Raton Club. His visit to Bonnet House in the early 1930s revealed that the ocean's salt spray was preventing the growth of almost everything except the coastal vegetation of palmettos and low scrub plants. He advised that a double row of Australian pines be planted

AERIAL OF BONNET HOUSE PROPERTY IN FORT LAUDERDALE.
CIRCA 1940.

along the eastern edge of the oceanfront dune (along A-1-A) to catch the salt spray. He also recommended that the sandy courtyard be removed to a depth of four feet and replaced with layers of marl, peat, and good topsoil.[7] Once his advice was followed, the property adapted to the choices of its owners and took on a lush, tropical personality.

During the execution of the master plan to create the Intracoastal Waterway, Frederic granted the Corps of Engineers permission to deposit the fill from their dredging operation on the western portion of the Bonnet House property in the late 1920s. Much of the established mangrove and buttonwood swamp perished, but Frederic Bartlett made the best of it. After he and Evelyn had pushed over the dead

trees, he developed a precise plan for a coconut plantation. Rows and rows of coconut palms were planted, and as they grew, so did the privacy from the increasing number of boaters motoring by on the Intracoastal "canal."

The Bartletts kept their own boat in the boathouse built in the center of the property on the canal dredged to the east of the Intracoastal. Originally the entrance point for delivery of materials during construction, the canal provided private access to the waterfront city of Fort Lauderdale. As restaurants and homes cropped up along the rivers and canals, their boat named "Bonnet" (a twenty-nine-foot Richardson) provided transportation via the New River inland to leisurely tour the city. Other than occasional trips along the coast by car or boating excursions, the Bartletts savored their time spent at Bonnet House. Shells brought home from the beaches began to appear throughout the residence, inlaid in concrete or carefully arranged in personal collections.

Expressions of endearment between the artist and his wife continued to fill their lives together. Frederic designed the shell museum complex, including an orchid house, bamboo bar, and circular shell museum for Evelyn as a gift. Featuring her favorite things, the shells, orchids and an intimate place to share with friends, the complex provides a most enchanting memory for all who visit. With close friendships playing a more important role than any offered by society, the gatherings at Bonnet House have been kept small. As occasions warranted, other structures were designed for different parts of the property. A stone fountain at the south allee was added as a focal point. Here, the south allee ended and the natural hammock of trees served as a backdrop. Not far from this statement of formality, next to a small pond, is the almost circus-like blue and gold striped pavilion built as a setting for outdoor social hours. At the opposite end of the lagoon, a theatre was built in order to show a movie about an African gorilla hunt by the Bartletts' Belgian friend, Armand Denis. Even a ticket booth was built for the event, and similar booths were used as portable pavilions in places when appropriate to the occasion.

ONCE ON A CAROUSEL, NOW AT BONNET HOUSE.

As host and hostess, the Bartletts have always radiated graciousness. Guests are invited to observe the most recent orchid blossoms, shells from around the world, and to share in the tranquil environment. Interrupted only by the sounds of the monkeys or birds, the peacefulness of Bonnet House has been deeply rooted in its owners. Their surroundings, enhanced by personal choice of design, color and content, tell an outer story of great inner detail. Service of a meal prepared by the Bartletts' chef, may best define this unique style which begins with a menu selected by Evelyn Bartlett. Planned in detail, the tableware, linen and centerpiece are coordinated with the food and the persons partaking of the meal. China selection comes from a dining room and pantry filled with a variety of patterns from which the lady of the house chooses. Even when china patterns are intermingled, their designs relate to the linen, crystal and silverware in the same conscious, colorful order found in her paintings. From the Rangpur lime cocktail, made from the limes grown on the property to finger bowls at dinner's end, a meal at Bonnet House is remembered in the flavor of its artistry.

For twenty-two years, Frederic and Evelyn Bartlett enjoyed a marriage and lifestyle of creative expression. Frederic Clay Bartlett's death in 1953, ended a well-traveled artistic life which began at the World's Columbian Exposition in 1893. His years with Evelyn Fortune Bartlett revived the enthusiasm he first had as an art student. From their European honeymoon to the home environments that flowered through the years, the Bartletts emanated an individual style untainted by society's trends or imposed

DINING AT THE BARTLETTS' RESIDENCE COMBINES AN ELEGANT TABLE SETTING WITH THE
CHEF'S DELECTABLE MEAL IN A GARDEN ATMOSPHERE.

———

expectations. Their collections mirror the places they visited and the friends who visited them; their lifestyle represents an appreciation for talent in the world and in themselves; and their concern, like that of Hugh Taylor Birch, has been for protecting the life and places where beauty is found.

In 1943, Mr. Birch died at the age of ninety-four, just two years following the deed-ing of his one hundred eighty acres north of Bonnet House as a state park. In his lifetime, he had given away seventeen hundred sixty acres of land in an effort "to preserve wildlife and natural woodland wherever he could."[8] What is imprinted from all of their lives is a legacy from which the world may learn the benefit of preserving the beauty, talent and commitment in one's daily life with love and care.

———

DINING BY CANDLELIGHT.

THE MARSHLAND EAST OF THE RESIDENCE WAS TRANSFORMED INTO A LAGOON. CIRCA 1932.

—

YOUNG GIRL IN THE
OSCEOLA FAMILY ASSISTED WITH THE
THATCHED ROOF OF THE BRIDGE.

—

BRIDGE PROVIDES PASSAGE FROM THE HOME ACROSS THE LAGOON TO THE BEACH.

ROYAL PALMS, PURCHASED WITH A BIRTHDAY CHECK FROM HER FATHER, WERE ADDED BY
EVELYN BARTLETT TO THE WESTERN SHORE OF THE LAGOON. CIRCA 1936.

PALMS CAREFULLY INTERWOVEN BY LOCAL INDIAN FAMILY MAKE A SECURE TROPICAL ROOF.

The focal point of the south allée is enhanced by marble creations from a place of the past.

CALCULATED DRAWINGS FOR
ALLÉE "FOUNTAIN" AND FLANKING COLUMNS SHOW
FREDERIC BARTLETT'S DESIGN.

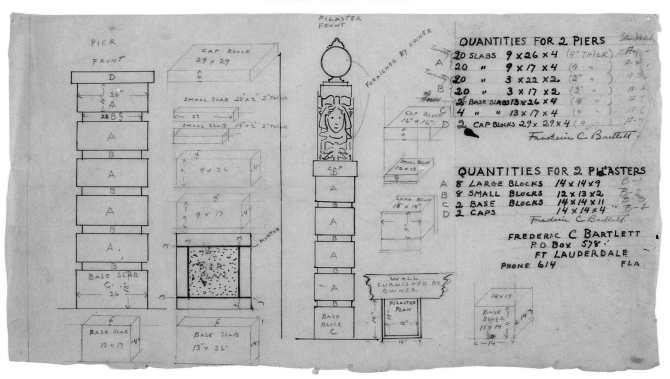

THE SHELL MUSEUM COMPLEX IS ADORNED WITH THE EAGLE,
A CONSISTENT THEME IN THE PLACES CREATED BY FREDERIC BARTLETT.

LOOKING UP AT PAINTED PINEAPPLES WITH COPPER LEAVES.

THE ORCHID HOUSE IS HOME FOR THE BLOOMING ORCHIDS FROM A COLLECTION OF MORE THAN TWO THOUSAND PLANTS.

CIRCULAR SHELL MUSEUM HOUSES SHELLS FROM AROUND THE WORLD,
ENHANCED BY DECORATIVE BORDERS FROM THE HAND OF FREDERIC BARTLETT.

———

BAMBOO BAR WAS SO PRECISELY PLANNED
THAT ONLY TWO STALKS OF BAMBOO
REMAINED WHEN COMPLETED.
AN INTIMATE SETTING FOR COCKTAILS.

A COCKTAIL MADE WITH THE RANGPUR LIME IS
THE FAVORED DRINK AT BONNET HOUSE. PEN AND INK
BY FREDERIC BARTLETT.

ISLAND THEATRE, SURROUNDED BY A MOAT, WAS RECONSTRUCTED IN 1987.

CLAY BARTLETT'S WATERCOLOR OF THE ISLAND THEATRE, 1944.

THEATRE WAS ORIGINALLY BUILT TO SHOW A MOVIE
ABOUT A GORILLA HUNT.

(ABOVE) METAL CIGARETTE BOX,
PAINTED BY EVIE LILLY, INSPIRED THE OIL PAINTING
BY FREDERIC BARTLETT
ABOVE THE DRAWING ROOM'S MANTEL.

(RIGHT) HANDCARVED GROUNDHOG FROM
ST. MORITZ HAS HIS NOSE RUBBED EVERY DAY BY
EVELYN BARTLETT FOR GOOD LUCK.

DRAWING ROOM, BUILT WITH MAHOGANY CEILING MADE FROM A LOG FOUND ON THE BEACH AND A FLOOR OF OJUS TILES MADE TO LOOK LIKE MARBLE, IS FILLED WITH OBJECTS THE BARTLETTS HAVE COLLECTED.

———

PORTRAIT OF CLAY BARTLETT BY HIS
FATHER. CERAMIC SCHOOL OF FISH
BELOW MADE BY EVELYN BARTLETT'S
DAUGHTER, EVIE.

————

PORTRAIT OF JEFF LOCKHART,
CARETAKER AND FRIEND OF
MR. BIRCH, BY FREDERIC BARTLETT.
CERAMIC BEARDED BUST IS
REMINISCENT OF HUGH TAYLOR BIRCH.

————

THE LOCATION OF THE BOATHOUSE IN THE CENTER OF THE PROPERTY HAS BEEN THE ACCESS POINT TO THE WATERWAYS
OF FORT LAUDERDALE SINCE BONNET HOUSE WAS BUILT IN 1920.

LOOKING THROUGH THE BOATHOUSE, THE PRIVATE CANAL LINED
WITH MANGROVES LEADS TO THE INTRACOASTAL WATERWAY.
HARDWARE FOR LIFTING BOATS HAS CHANGED THROUGH THE YEARS.

———

1938 Case tractor was purchased by Evelyn Bartlett
in the 1950s to aid the caretaker with his tasks.
For decades, the role of groundskeeper, caretaker and
gardener was carried out by one man.

———

THE WORKSHOP PROVIDED THE PLACE FOR FREDERIC BARTLETT
TO COMPLETE HIS DESIGNS FOR BENCHES, TABLES
AND OTHER DECORATIVE ELEMENTS. ONCE HE HAD MADE THE
PROTOTYPE, A CARPENTER WOULD OFTEN ASSIST IN MAKING
DUPLICATES OF HIS ORIGINAL.

———

PAVILION FACING THE SOUTH LILY POND WAS THE IDEAL SETTING FOR MR. BARTLETT'S MURAL OF A PRINCESS ON A PINK ELEPHANT.
THE BONNET LILY OUTSIDE IS A REMINDER OF THE NAME FOR BONNET HOUSE.

PORTABLE PAVILIONS WERE USED ON THE PROPERTY WHEN DEEMED APPROPRIATE.

EARLY DAYS AT THE SOUTH POND. CIRCA 1940.

AGAVE STRETCHES ITS ARMS TO THE SUN.

A DESERT OF SPECIMEN PALMS AND SUCCULENTS SPANS THE SAND
AT THE SOUTH ENTRANCE. THE DESERT ENVIRONMENT IS
MAINTAINED AS INTENDED BY FREDERIC AND EVELYN BARTLETT.

GALLERY OF EVELYN BARTLETT'S WATERCOLORS IN A FORMER
GUEST WING AT BONNET HOUSE.

———

———

OF EVELYN BARTLETT'S OILS ON CANVAS, THE PORTRAIT OF HER HUSBAND AND DAUGHTER CAPTURES MANY AN EYE AND HEART.

———

SILVER PALM — FLORIDA TABLE — WATERCOLOR BY EVELYN BARTLETT.

A POPULAR RESIDENT AT BONNET HOUSE, THE BRAZILIAN SQUIRREL MONKEY GLADLY RECEIVES FRESH PEANUTS.

———

SET OF PLATES, CANISTERS AND TUREEN, MADE AND PAINTED BY EVELYN BARTLETT'S DAUGHTER, EVIE LILLY.

———

FISH, SHELLS AND TURTLE WERE PAINTED BY FREDERIC BARTLETT WHEN HE ASKED HIS WIFE TO ADD THE NETTING.

1941 CADILLAC FOUR-DOOR, CONVERTIBLE, ONE OF 400 MADE, IS BEING RESTORED
TO ITS ORIGINAL CONDITION.

———

(ABOVE) ENTRANCE HALL AT WHITEHALL INTRODUCES FAMILIAR THEMES: THE EAGLE, OBELISKS AND PATTERNED FLOOR.
(RIGHT) OBELISKS AT BOTHWAYS FARM.

OTHER SPECIAL PLACES

With Bonnet House as a winter residence, other homes served important purposes to the Bartletts throughout the year. The south Florida climate influenced their return to the north each spring and provided seasonal beauty and comfort through the following autumn. Whitehall, their residence in Beverly, Massachusetts, is situated on top of a rocky bluff and overlooks the ocean on the north shore of Boston. Designed by the Boston firm of Little & Browne Architects, the former Francis I. Amory estate was purchased by Hugh Taylor Birch and Frederic Bartlett in the spring of 1925. The three-story Georgian-style mansion amidst the treetops provided a more formal home on which Frederic Bartlett would leave his mark.

The death of Helen Birch Bartlett occurred just months after the home had been purchased. For the next five years, Frederic and his son, Clay, continued to share their spring, summer and fall seasons at Whitehall with Mr. Birch when they were not traveling. When artistic inspiration was revived within Frederic, design elements that appealed to him began to surface: obelisks were created and surfaces marbleized; patterned floors and carpets interacted with painted surfaces and gilded trim; and sculpture collected on foreign excursions was placed in a symmetrical garden design.

At the base of the rocky bluff, Frederic converted an old three-story building into his art studio. By removing a ceiling and second floor, he created a two-story high room where he installed a large north window to provide the perfect light in which to paint. Later, the building was expanded with a large addition providing two galleries for works to be hung and selectively

ART STUDIO AND GALLERY IN BEVERLY PROVIDED AN IDEAL PLACE TO WORK AND DISPLAY WORKS OF ART.

shown. The location of the studio-gallery complex on a public street from which the climbing entrance drive to the house begins, made it easily accessible to those invited to attend private showings. Skylit ceilings in the galleries, a sound system to keep the music playing, and a neutral gray interior contributed to the ideal ambiance for private art openings. With four artists in the family, Frederic and his son, Clay, and Evelyn and her daughter, Evie, a family show offered great variety.

Transformation of life in Beverly may well be equated with the blossoming of Bonnet House. The marriage of Evelyn Fortune Lilly and Frederic Bartlett in 1931, brought new life into Whitehall as it was prepared to be their home. Ever fond of his "splendid son-in-law"[1] and new bride, Mr. Birch changed his summer address to Yellow Springs, Ohio, but continued to share the winter residence of Bonnet House to remain close to the people he loved. Frederic painted a portrait of Evelyn which was hung in the drawing room at Whitehall. His transformation of a porch into a long, narrow gallery reflects the gallery hall built in the home of Frederic's father in Lake Geneva, Wisconsin, decades earlier. The small round room at one end of the gallery with its patterned floor and carved frieze is a reminder of the shell museum built for Evelyn at Bonnet House.

Fabrics and formalities go hand-in-hand in the well-endowed lifestyles of New England interiors. Whitehall presents itself elegantly. Carpets edged with marbleized borders painted on the floor, and wallpaper painted with drapery festoons hint at the draped fabric in the formal dining room. These expressions of an artist whose sense of humor was often "tongue in cheek," made artistic statements incongruous with the "proper" formal style. The personal freedom in embellishing life with such delight makes the life of Frederic Bartlett one of original style, carried through in everything he touched.

In 1938, the perimeters for creativity were extended when Evelyn Bartlett purchased

PORTRAIT OF EVELYN FORTUNE BARTLETT BY FREDERIC BARTLETT. 1931.

a farm in the neighboring community of Essex, Massachusetts. Having belonged to a family who raised poultry and cultivated flowers, the farm fulfilled a desire that Evelyn had shared with her daughter; to own a farm. Named "Bothways Farm" for its view of the water from either side (in the early days) and for its two entrances, the one hundred fourteen acre farm has nurtured a healthy life for Evelyn Bartlett who has lived beyond one hundred years. Growing her own vegetables and fruits, raising cattle, sheep, and a great variety of poultry, and enjoying the fresh dairy riches of cream, milk and butter, provides a secure source for genuine nutrition. Her love of flower arranging is supported by an expansive flower garden of dahlias, lilies, sweet peas, and in the greenhouse, carnations, chrysanthemums, snapdragons, and begonias. Many other varieties are intermixed, and all are specially selected by Evelyn Bartlett.

Like the other Bartlett properties, the talents and sensitivities of Frederic and Evelyn are found throughout the farm. The custom-mixed yellow paint adorns the houses for the ducks, swans and chickens as well as the barns, farmhouses and fences. It is the original color of the buildings as Evelyn found them. Carousel animals perched on fenceposts outside the barn repeat Frederic Bartlett's menagerie of carved animals also found at Bonnet House and at Whitehall. Obelisks, a constant in Mr. Bartlett's repertoire of design, stand at the end of paths in the vegetable garden. When one realizes the riches of the farm, there is little wonder that the sense of purpose found in Bothways Farm coincided with Evelyn Bartlett's decision to cease painting. Both she and her husband found a new source of pleasure in the pastures, garden and hillside in Essex.

A pinnacle of mutual delight at Bothways Farm revolved around the celebration

WHITEHALL'S "ROUND ROOM" WAS ADDED TO THE ORIGINAL RESIDENCE AND INCLUDES A CARVED FRIEZE AND PATTERNED FLOOR.

honoring Evelyn, and the works of "Mr. Currier and Mr. Ives." For six weeks prior to the party on August 23, 1946, Frederic worked diligently on the hill creating banners, painting his interpretation of several Currier and Ives prints, and arranging a grand entrance through which guests would arrive. His efforts were kept a secret, even from Evelyn. Folding screens painted with classical garden scenery were positioned in a circle as a backdrop for the fully-catered party in the woods. Entertainment was provided in the barn, the Currier and Ives paintings were "unveiled" in the little picnic house, and cocktails were served from a festively-painted bar. When the host of guests

were seated for lunch, the grand event was visited by rain. Although umbrellas went up and all continued to enjoy the party, Frederic was determined never to have rain interfere with another party.

His plans for a hunting lodge on top of the hill were immediately begun. Recalling the Bavarian settings in the forests he so loved outside of Munich, Frederic designed the Bothways Hunting Lodge to fit his entertainment needs. A pair of deer painted on the lodge's hanging sign and doors symbolizes the origin of the hunting lodge. Yet, there are roosters inside the intimate bar. Gilded American eagles, a portrait of Napoleon, and arched panels with fife and drum embellish the formal dining room that may, at first, surprise a guest. Meant for a different kind of enchantment is the chapel, designed with a European flair. Upon entering the chapel down the steps from the Hunt-

ing Lodge, guests are greeted by a carved wooden stag wearing a fresh flower garland for all social gatherings. Each of the buildings that Frederic Bartlett created, including the picnic house, adds to the indefatigable originality that emanated from his life.

The same freedom that allows an artist to sample every style of expression incites an adventurous spirit. To create a place like Nymphenglade in the wilds of the Florida Everglades proves that Frederic Bartlett's imag-

ination worked anywhere. He had in mind a beautiful Royal hunting lodge in Bavaria called Nymphenburg. He made the exterior of Nymphenglade rather elegant but the interior cozy and peasant-like. The bed was built in one corner of the single large room. It was enclosed in curtains which could be pulled open or closed like those around peasant beds in earlier days. Frederic Bartlett drew a master plan for the entire acreage: statuary was positioned about the lawn; obelisks were interspersed along the entrance drive; and a fruit grove was planted behind the residence. Located thirteen miles west of Fort Lauderdale in Davie, Nymphenglade was an overnight retreat for the Bartletts. Although Mrs. Bartlett was not fond of the snakes they found on their property, they continued to drive to Nymphenglade until gas rationing prevented their doing so during World War II.

During the 1947 hurricane, the home and its contents were severely damaged. The following year the Bartletts sold their retreat in the Everglades. The ceiling paintings from the living room and a sampling of sculpture were salvaged by Evelyn Bartlett to be placed in the courtyard of Bonnet House.

Space surrounding a residence may well contribute to the sense of its being in a world all its own. In each home environment they have shared, the Bartletts have enjoyed a world of privacy and individuality. Their very selection of locations in which to live reflects an appreciation for a botanically affluent setting that interrelates with the architecture of the home and the lifestyle of its owners. The personal dedication to quality in life shines through the life and works of both Frederic and Evelyn Bartlett.

ORIGINAL BLUEPRINT FOR NYMPHENGLADE DRAWN BY FREDERIC BARTLETT.

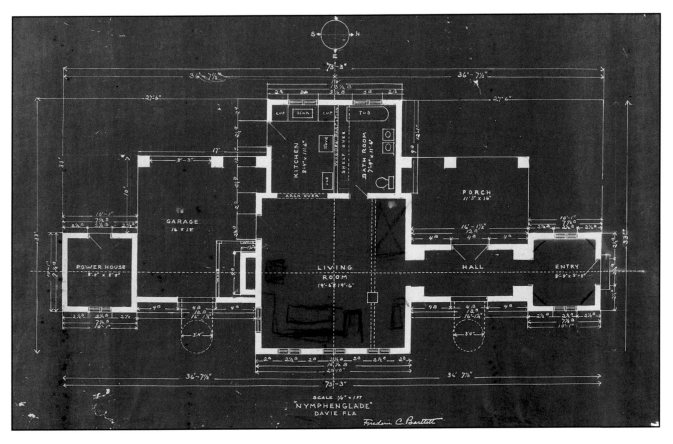

NYMPHENGLADE, INSPIRED BY THE GERMAN CASTLE OF NYMPHENBURG, WAS THE BARTLETTS' WEEKEND RETREAT NEAR THE EDGE OF THE FLORIDA EVERGLADES.

OBELISKS LINING THE ENTRANCE DRIVE WERE PART OF MR. BARTLETT'S MASTER PLAN FOR THE GROUNDS AND RESIDENCE.

A COZY, PEASANTLIKE INTERIOR ECHOES A EUROPEAN STYLE
SO LOVED BY FREDERIC BARTLETT. THE CEILING PANELS
WERE LATER BROUGHT TO BONNET HOUSE.

WHITEHALL, THE BIRCH-BARTLETT HOME IN BEVERLY, MASSACHUSETTS, PURCHASED IN 1925.

THE TIERED GARDEN ON THE HILLSIDE AT WHITEHALL
WAS DESIGNED BY FREDERIC BARTLETT.

———

A FORMER PORCH WAS ENCLOSED TO CREATE THE FORMAL GALLERY WITH FEATURES SIMILAR TO
THE GALLERY HALL AT "HOUSE IN THE WOODS."

DRAWING ROOM AT WHITEHALL IS A BLEND OF TREASURES FROM THE BIRCH-BARTLETT FAMILY.

ROSE GARDEN WAS EVELYN BARTLETT'S ADDITION TO WHITEHALL.

HUNTING LODGE INTERIOR.

A HINT OF BAVARIA ON A HILL IN ESSEX, MASSACHUSETTS—FREDERIC BARTLETT'S
HUNTING LODGE AT BOTHWAYS FARM.

PICNIC HOUSE AT BOTHWAYS FARM HOUSES THE CURRIER
AND IVES PAINTINGS COMPLETED IN 1946.

———

AMERICAN THEMES MAKE A TRADITIONAL STATEMENT FROM THE BRUSH OF A VERSATILE ARTIST.

THE CARVED WOODEN STAG GREETS ANYONE GOING TO THE CHAPEL AT BOTHWAYS FARM.

A PAIR OF CARVED WOODEN ROOSTERS SEEM A PERFECT INTRODUCTION TO
THE POULTRY "QUARTERS" UP THE HILL.

————

————

MR. BARTLETT EVEN DESIGNED THE BIRDHOUSE.

————

YOUNG CALF IS ONE
OF THE BEEF CATTLE—JERSEYS
ARE RAISED FOR DAIRY.

LLAMAS AND EMUS WERE ADDED
TO THE FAMILY IN THE 1980S.

A MIXED BREED CALLED "TOPHATS" ARE ON THE FARM "FOR FUN."

A VARIETY OF JULY LILIES SELECTED BY EVELYN BARTLETT.

———

(ABOVE) MY DRESSING TABLE BY EVELYN FORTUNE BARTLETT. CIRCA 1933.
(RIGHT) EVELYN BARTLETT WITH HER YORKSHIRE TERRIER, HONEY. CIRCA 1945.

A Tribute

A personal set of principles stems from one's background and experiences, along with a commitment to living as one believes. Frederic and Evelyn Bartlett have expressed their love of life in the way they have spent their time—together or individually. The lifestyle they have so generously shared with friends is more than just a sparkling memory. It is also a reminder of the capacity that each person holds for keeping joy a part of everyday life.

Evelyn Fortune Bartlett witnessed the success of her father in the contributions he made to the world. A preservationist ahead of his time, William Fortune purchased the home of the great poet, James Whitcomb Riley, to ensure that it would one day be properly preserved. Evelyn, following in his footsteps, has had the foresight to commemorate the beloved people, places and beauty in her life.

Although 1953 marks the end of Frederic Bartlett's life, Evelyn Bartlett has continued to pay tribute to his talents as a person and an artist. Her private printing in 1965 of his *Sortofa Kindofa Journal of My Own*, written in the early years of their marriage, has provided a window to the heart and soul of a man whose life blossomed in its exposure to the arts in cultures around the world. In 1982, the Smithsonian Institution held a retrospective showing of selected paintings by Frederic and Evelyn Bartlett. The exhibit's gallery display and accompanying text paid tribute to the artistic accomplishments of both artists and reinforced their significance as would be memorialized at Bonnet House. Evelyn Bartlett's gift of Bonnet House in 1983, was the largest single philanthropic gift in the state of Florida to date. While a selection of the Bartletts' paintings will

A WOMAN OF GREAT RESPONSIBILITY HANDLES HER PERSONAL AFFAIRS IN A METICULOUS FASHION.

remain at the Indianapolis Art Museum, the Corcoran Gallery, the Carnegie Institute, the Art Institute of Chicago and in private collections, the majority of their works are featured at Bonnet House.

Knowing Frederic's desire to have the Helen Birch-Bartlett Memorial Collection of Post-Impressionist paintings kept in one room at the Art Institute of Chicago, Evelyn worked diligently to honor his wish. With the assistance of Mr. William Blair, former Chairman of the Art Institute's Board of Trustees, an appropriate location was found. Due to the dedication of Evelyn Bartlett, the collection of world-famous paintings housed in the Frederic Clay Bartlett Memorial Gallery will remain in a place of prominence.

Evelyn Fortune Bartlett's generous gift of Bonnet House and her contribution to *Reflections of a Legacy*, provide future generations with the opportunity to realize the beauty revered in the lives of Frederic and Evelyn Bartlett. The romanticism which permeates their art, their residences and the simple pleasures of their lives, touches the heart and soul of everyone who takes notice.

EVELYN BARTLETT IS ADORNED IN YELLOW SILK STRIPED IN BLACK VELVET FOR HER DAUGHTER'S
DEBUTANTE PARTY IN 1938.

SITTING AREA IN THE STUDY AT WHITEHALL.

"YESTERDAY-TODAY-TOMORROW,"
FLOWERING SHRUB INTRODUCED
AT BONNET HOUSE BY
EVELYN BARTLETT IN HER
ONE HUNDREDTH YEAR.

EVELYN BARTLETT WITH HER PAPILLON, ABBEY. 1989.

AFTERWORD

*E*velyn Fortune Bartlett has been blessed with good health for more than one hundred years. A grand celebration was given at Bothways Farm in honor of her one-hundredth birthday, September 30, 1987. Outdoors, beneath the pines, the stone-outlined circle where Frederic had given her a party in 1946 was graced by towering sunflowers in its center. Tables adorned with bright yellow cloths and large, colorful heads of kale pouring forth an array of flowers, set the stage for the Lady of Honor to arrive in her horse-drawn carriage. An organ grinder and his monkey, strolling musicians, and one hundred special guests shared in the sunlit gaiety of a most memorable day.

ENDNOTES

Chapter 2. A Sense of Time and Place.

1. Joan Runkel, "Dusty Records." *Inside Whitehall.* March-April 1984, vol. 1. no. 4.
2. Ibid.
3. David Leon Chandler, *Henry Flagler: The Astonishing Life and Times of the Visionary Robber Baron Who Founded Florida.* (New York, 1986), pp. 127-130.
4. Evelyn Bartlett, Personal interview with Raymond George. 25 October 1977.
5. Bertram Zuckerman, *The Dream Lives On: A History of Fairchild Tropical Garden 1938-1988* (Miami, 1988), p. 21.
6. Hugh Taylor Birch, Letter to Mr. Fairchild. 15 December 1924.
7. Hap Hatton, *Tropical Splendor: An Architectural History of Florida* (New York, 1987), p. 60.
8. Hugh Taylor Birch, Letter to Mr. Fairchild, 29 July 1926.
9. Lucy G. Morgan, *The Story of Glen Helen.* (Yellow Springs, Ohio, 1931).
10. Morgan.
11. Courtney Graham Donnell, "Frederic Clay and Helen Birch Bartlett: The Collectors." *The Art Institute of Chicago Museum Studies.* Vol. 12, No. 2, (Chicago, 1986), p. 89.
12. Morgan.
13. Ibid.
14. "A.C. Bartlett," *Chicago Tribune* 9 Sept. 1900, p. 38.
15. Frederic Clay Bartlett, *Sortofa Kindofa Journal of My Own,* (Chicago, 1965), p. 32.
16. Evelyn Bartlett, Personal interview with Raymond George, 25 October 1977.
17. Hatton, p. 35.
18. Hatton, pp. 80-81.
19. "Medieval Castle at Las Olas," *Fort Lauderdale Sentinel* 11 July 1921, p.1.
20. Hugh Taylor Birch, Letter to Mr. Fairchild. 20 April 1927.

Chapter 3. A Talent Established.

1. Henry Austin Dobson, *Ars Victrix*, st. 8, (passage in the entrance lobby of the Fine Arts Building of Chicago).
2. Frederic Clay Bartlett, *Sortofa Kindofa Journal of My Own.* p. 4.
3. Ibid.
4. David G. Lowe, "When Everyone Knew What He Liked." *The Nineties* (New York, 1967), p. 65.
5. Ibid.
6. George Heard Hamilton, "Painting and Sculpture in Europe 1880-1940." *The Pelican History of Art.* (Baltimore, 1967), p. 15.
7. Anne Cannon Palumbo, "The Paintings of Frederic Clay Bartlett and Evelyn Fortune Bartlett." Smithsonian Institution, 1982.

8. Florence and Erne R. Freuh, "Frederic Clay Bartlett: Chicago Painter and Patron of the Arts." *Chicago History* Spring 1979, p. 16.
9. Bartlett, pp. 51-52.
10. Ibid. p. 64.
11. Donnell, p. 86.
12. *Chicago Tribune.* 11 March 1906.
13. Freuh, p. 17.
14. Donnell, p. 87.
15. Freuh, p. 17.
16. "Country House in the West," *Ladies Home Journal.* June 1909.
17. Freuh, p. 17.
18. Ibid.
19. "F.C. Bartlett, Noted Chicagoan Artist, Dies," *Chicago Daily Tribune.* 26 June 1953.

Chapter 4. Influence in Harmony.

1. Helen Birch Bartlett, *Capricious Winds.* (Boston, New York, 1927), intro by Janet Fairbanks, p. xiii.
2. Donnell, p. 90.
3. Morgan.
4. Evelyn Bartlett, Personal interview with Raymond George. 25 October 1977.
5. Richard R. Brettell, "The Bartlett's and the Grande Jatte: Collecting Modern Painting in the 1920's." *The Art Institute of Chicago Museum Studies.* Vol. 12, No. 2, (Chicago, 1986), p. 104.
6. Donnell, p. 94.
7. Brettell, p. 104.
8. Ibid, p. 106.
9. Ibid., p. 109.
10. Ibid.
11. Ibid, pp. 111-112.

Chapter 5. A Commitment Nurtured.

1. Lucille E. Morehouse, "Discovery Wife was Artist Most Successful Venture." *Indianapolis Star* 11 April 1934.
2. Thalia, (an Indianapolis newspaper), 1 June 1931.
3. *The Travel Agent*, June 1937.
4. Morehouse.
5. Frederic Bartlett, "Paintings by Evelyn Bartlett." Catalogue for John Heron Art Museum Exhibit 8-29 April 1934.
6. Evelyn Bartlett, Personal interview with Raymond George, 25 October 1977.
7. Ibid.
8. *The Springfield News-Sun.* (Springfield, Ohio) 17 January 1943.

Chapter 6. Other Special Places.

1. Donnell, p. 91.

WORKS CITED

"A.C. Bartlett." *Chicago Tribune* 9 September 1900, p. 38.

"A Country House in the West." *Ladies Home Journal* June 1909.

"A Tribute to Florence Dibell Bartlett." The Museum of International Folk Art, Santa Fe, New Mexico 5 Sept. 1963.

Arnold, C.D. and H.D. Higinbotham. *The World's Columbian Exposition, Portfolio of Views.* Department of Photography, C.B. Woodward Company, St. Louis, 1893.

Bartlett, Evelyn Fortune. Personal interview with Raymond George. 25 October 1977.

Bartlett, Frederic. "Paintings by Evelyn Bartlett." Catalogue for John Heron Art Museum Exhibit 8-29, April 1934.

Bartlett, Frederic Clay. *Sortofa Kindofa Journal of My Own.* Chicago: Donnelly, 1965.

Bartlett, Helen Birch. *Capricious Winds.* Boston and New York, 1927. Introduction by Janet Fairbank, p. xiii.

Birch, Hugh Taylor. Letter to Mr. David Fairchild. 15 December 1924. Montgomery Library. Fairchild Tropical Garden.

Birch, Hugh Taylor. Letter to Mr. David Fairchild. 29 July 1926. Montgomery Library. Fairchild Tropical Garden.

Birch, Hugh Taylor. Letter to Mr. David Fairchild. 20 April 1927. Montgomery Library. Fairchild Tropical Garden.

Brettell, Richard R. "The Bartlett's and the Grande Jatte: Collecting Modern Painting in the 1920's." *The Art Institute of Chicago Museum Studies.* Volume 12, No. 2, 1986.

Burgan, Beatrice. "Paintings Show Joy of Living." *Indianapolis Times* 12 April 1934.

Chandler, David Leon. *Henry Flagler: The Astonishing Life and Times of the Visionary Robber Baron Who Founded Florida.* New York, 1986.

Chicago Tribune (Dorfred House) 11 March 1906.

Cunningham, Inez. "Long Awaited Show of Religious Art Opens." *The Chicago Evening Post.* 24 March 1931.

Donnell, Courtney Graham. "Frederic Clay and Helen Birch Bartlett: The Collectors." *The Art Institute of Chicago Museum Studies.* Vol. 12, No. 2, 1986.

"F.C. Bartlett, 80, Artist Collector." *New York Times* 26 June 1953, p. 19.

"Fort Lauderdale's First Citizen: Frank Stranahan..." *Fort Lauderdale Daily News.* 4 August 1925.

Freuh, Florence and Erne R. "Frederic Clay Bartlett: Chicago Painter and Patron of the Arts." *Chicago History* Spring 1979.

Goodspeed, Thomas Wakefield. "Adolphus Clay Bartlett." *The University of Chicago Biographical Sketches.* Vol. II, 1925: pp. 100-123.

Hamilton, George Heard. *The Pelican History of Art: Painting and Sculpture in Europe 1880-1940.* Ed. Nikolaus Peysner. Baltimore, Md.: Penguin Books, Inc., 1967.

Hatton, Hap. *Tropical Splendor: An Architectural History of Florida.* New York: Alfred A. Knopf, 1987.

Hortt, M.A. *Gold Coast Pioneer,* New York: Exposition Press, 1953.

Lowe, David G. "When Everyone Knew What He Liked." *The Nineties.* New York: American Heritage Publishing Co., Inc., 1967.

"Medieval Castle at Las Olas." *Fort Lauderdale Sentinel* 11 July 1921. p. 1.

McGoun, Bill. "A Biographic History of Broward County." *Miami Herald.* 1972.

Morehouse, Lucille E. *Indianapolis Star.* 11 April 1934.

Morgan, Joy Elmer. *Horace Mann at Antioch.* The Horace Mann Centennial Fund. Washington, D.C.: 1938.

Morgan, Lucy G., comp. *The Story of Glen Helen.* Yellow Springs, OH: The Antioch Press, 1931.

Osborn, Margaret. "Cast Iron Artisan," *Americana* Vol. 14, Sept.- Oct. 1986. pp. 34-39.

Palumbo, Anne Cannon, "The Paintings of Frederic Clay Bartlett and Evelyn Fortune Bartlett." Smithsonian Institution Exhibit Leaflet. 17 Sept. - 17 Nov. 1982.

Roberts, Edward F. "Adolphus C. Bartlett, Merchant Prince. Adheres to Simple Rules of Life." *Chicago Tribune* 25 October 1908.

Runkle, Joan, "Dusty Records." *Inside Whitehall*, March-April 1984, Vol. 1. No. 4.

Thalia, (an Indianapolis newspaper). 1 June 1931.

The Travel Agent, June 1937.

"The Reading of the Minutes." University Club of Chicago Golden Anniversary Jubilee, 11 Feb. 1937, pp. 39-43.

Warren, Pauline. "Ritz Carlton is Transformed for Glittering Debutante Party." *The Boston Herald* 11 November 1937.

Weeks, Francis Dickin. "A Gothic Chase and Feast. " *Seventy-Six, The University Club of Chicago.* Spring 1981.

———. "Development of Stained Glass Windows." *Seventy- Six, The University Club of Chicago.* April 1977.

———. "Themes and Details of 14 Stained Glass Windows." *Seventy-Six, The University Club of Chicago.* May 1977.

———. "Tribute to Frederic C. Bartlett." *Seventy-Six, The University Club of Chicago.* May 1978.

———. "Stained Glass Windows: Cathedral Hall." Part 1, *Seventy-Six, The University Club of Chicago.* May 1982.

———. "Stained Glass Windows: Cathedral Hall." Part 2, *Seventy-Six, The University Club of Chicago.* June 1982.

———. "Stained Glass Windows: Cathedral Hall." Part 3, *Seventy-Six, The University Club of Chicago.* July 1982.

Smiley, Nixon, *Yesterday's Florida.* Miami: E.A. Seamann Publishing, Inc., 1974.

Weidling, Philip J. and August Burghard, *Checkered Sunshine, The Story of Fort Lauderdale 1793-1955.* Fort Lauderdale: Wake- Brook, 1974.

"William Fortune." *Cyclopedia of American Biography of the American Historical Society, Inc.,* Vol XXXIV. 1928.

Wolfmeyer, Ann and Mary Burns Gage. *Lake Geneva Newport of the West 1870-1920.* Vol. 1, Lake Geneva: 1976.

Zuckerman, Bertram. *The Dream Lives On: A History of Fairchild Tropical Garden 1938-1988.* Miami, 1988.

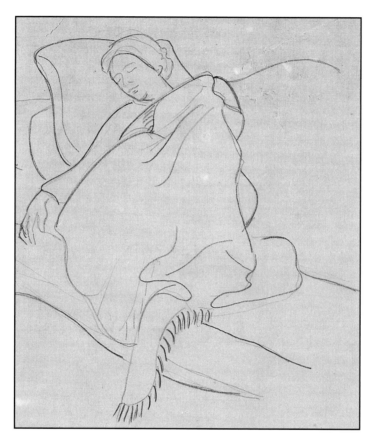

PENCIL SKETCH BY FREDERIC BARTLETT.

CREDITS

Photography

Courtesy of Antiochiana Collection, Antioch College pages 23, 68, 69.

©1989. The Art Institute of Chicago. All rights reserved. Pages 47 (lower right), 70, 71, 72, 73, 74, 75.

©Bonnet House Archives pages 24 (lower right), 25, 28, 29, 30, 31, 32, 39, 41 (top), 46 (upper right), 49, 50, 77, 78, 79 (lower left), 80, 82, 86, 87, 107, 120 (bottom), 122, 123, 141.

©Steven Brooke pages 16 (top), 33, 47 (upper right), 100, 116, 119, 124, 125, 126, 127, 135 (bottom), 136 (upper right, bottom), 142, 144 (top).

©Delaware State Archives page 24 (top).

©Don DuBroff page 54.

©Courtney Donnell page 47 (lower left).

Courtesy of The Henry M. Flagler Museum, Palm Beach, Florida. page 22.

©Steve Hall, Hedrich-Blessing pages 60, 61, 62, 63.

©Bill Hedrich, Hedrich-Blessing pages 55, 58, 59.

©Claudia Ogilvie pages 14 (top), 147.

©John D. Pearce page 10.

©Mike Purcell, Flamingo Gardens page 144 (bottom).

©Ralph Rinzler, Smithsonian Institution page 5.

Courtesy of Mr. and Mrs. Patrick Ryan page 52.

Courtesy of Elisabeth Bartlett Sturges page 143.

©Phillip C. Urion, University Club of Chicago pages 56, 57.

©Ray Weiner page 11.

All other photography — Tony Branco.

Editing

Jayme Robinson

Graphic Design and Production

William Armenteros and Linda Martin
Drexel & Ives, Inc.
Coral Gables, Florida

Printing

Haff-Daugherty Graphics, Inc.
Hialeah, Florida

Typography

BoldType, Inc.
Coral Gables, Florida